# *EA* FORGIVENESS

*Forgiving is not something that we do, but the effortless outcome of knowing the truth in our hearts.*

Ed M. Smith &
Joshua A. Smith

THIS BOOK IS AN INTRODUCTION TO THE PRINCIPLES OF
TRANSFORMATION PRAYER MINISTRY AND FORGIVENESS

Copyright © 2018 - New Creation Publishing, Campbellsville, KY

All rights reserved. No part of this publication may be reproduced, distributed, or transmitted in any form or by any means, including photocopying, recording, or other electronic or mechanical methods, without the prior written permission of the publisher, except in the case of brief quotations embodied in critical reviews and certain other noncommercial uses permitted by copyright law. For permission requests, send email to the publisher at **iatm@theophostic.com**

Unless otherwise specified, all Bible quotations are taken from the New American Standard Bible (NASV), Copyright 1960,1962, 1963, 1968, 1971, 1972, 1973, 1975, 1977, 1995 by the Lockman Foundation. All Bible quotations are used by permission.

Scripture quotations marked (NKJV) are taken from the New King James Version®. Copyright © 1982 by Thomas Nelson. Used by permission. All rights reserved.

Scripture quotations marked (NCV) are taken from the New Century Version®. Copyright © 2005 by Thomas Nelson. Used by permission. All rights reserved.

Scripture quotations marked (RSV) are taken from the Revised Standard Version of the Bible, copyright © 1946, 1952, and 1971 National Council of the Churches of Christ in the United States of America. Used by permission. All rights reserved.

Scripture quotations marked HCSB®, are taken from the Holman Christian Standard Bible®, Copyright © 1999, 2000, 2002, 2003, 2009 by Holman Bible Publishers. Used by permission. HCSB® is a federally registered trademark of Holman Bible Publishers.

Scripture quotations marked (NIV) are taken from the Holy Bible, New International Version®, NIV®. Copyright © 1973, 1978, 1984, 2011 by Biblica, Inc.™ Used by permission of Zondervan. All rights reserved worldwide. www.zondervan.com The "NIV" and "New International Version" are trademarks registered in the United States Patent and Trademark Office by Biblica, Inc.™

Some liberty has been taken in boldfacing, italicizing, and [bracketing] certain words and phrases in the biblical text for emphasis that may not have been included in the translator's copy.

Book Layout and Design by Andy Grachuk
www.JingotheCat.com

# Transformation Prayer Ministry (TPM)

The basic tenets of this book are based upon many of the principles found in the prayer ministry model Transformation Prayer Ministry (TPM). The TPM model is being used by tens of thousands of Christian counselors, pastors, church leaders, lay ministers as well as literally untold thousands of followers of Jesus Christ in over 200 countries worldwide. For more information and free training go to: www.transformationprayer.org

# Getting the Most Out of Your Time Investment

Most of us only read a book once. If the book does not provide any measurable benefit, then only reading it one time is more investment than our time was worth. However, if the book offers life changing truth, then retaining what we read is priceless. The problem is, very few of us will retain more than about 12-15% of what we read once and only then if we apply what we learn by making it a part of our daily lives.

Therefore, it would seem prudent to gain the most we can from our time investment. As you read this book we ask that you consider whether what you read is something that you want to remember and carry forward. If you determine that it has value and desire to retain it, then there are several things you might consider doing to increase your comprehension.

1. Read it again. If you will purpose to read this book a second time within a few weeks of your first reading, your retention rate will increase significantly.

2. Make note of what you are reading. During your first reading, keep a highlighter in your hand. Highlight the parts that you want to be sure to remember? Later, go back to those areas and read them over and again. You will be surprised how much more you will remember if you do this.

3. Consider reading this book with a friend or a small group. Have open discussions about the concepts and principles you learn together. Perhaps use this book in your church small group, but then encourage the group to repeat the study again later.

4. After reading each chapter go back and re-read, out loud, each *focal point* (the highlighted quotes found throughout each chapter) and ponder each one and purpose to remember it.

5. Consider approaching this book in the same way you would your Bible study. This book is by no means on the same level as the Bible, but you are reading it with the same mind and with the same rate of retention as when you study the Scriptures. No one would read the Bible one time through and assume that they understood all they read. We read the Scriptures over and over, digging out the treasures they afford us, nugget by nugget. If you find value in reading this book your first time through, consider reading it over and again to gain all that you can.

6. Use the "Discussion Questions" found at the end of each chapter to help determine if you comprehended what you read. If you are a part of a small group read each question out loud and allow for open discussion.

# Contents

INTRODUCTION: *Tight Jaws and Clenched Fists* — 11

CHAPTER ONE: *What is Transformation Prayer Ministry?* — 29

CHAPTER TWO: *Forgiving from the Heart* — 47

CHAPTER THREE: *Faith: The Persuasion of God* — 61

CHAPTER FOUR: *Principles of Forgiveness in Matthew 18* — 83

CHAPTER FIVE: Principle One: *Forgiveness requires that we assess the debt and take an account* — 93

CHAPTER SIX: *The Importance of Memory in Taking an Account* — 107

CHAPTER SEVEN: Principle Two: *The one who "owes" us does not have the means to repay the debt* — 121

CHAPTER EIGHT: Principle Three: *Anger is a normal reaction to injustice, but must be released before freedom will come* — 131

CHAPTER NINE: Principle Four: *Forgiveness has nothing to do with the attitude or cooperation of the one whose debt is being forgiven* — 143

CHAPTER TEN: Principle Five: *Genuine forgiveness requires that we have compassion* — 151

CHAPTER ELEVEN: Principle Six: *Forgiveness emotionally releases the one offering the forgiveness, but may have no impact on the one whose debt has been cleared* — 165

CHAPTER TWELVE: Principle Seven: *Forgiveness should not be confused with reconciliation* — 183

FINAL WORDS: *Forgiveness allows us to see the bigger picture* — 199

# Introduction

## Tight Jaws and Clenched Fists

Carla sat in my prayer room waiting for me to pray with her. Just looking at her, the tension was evident. She clenched her fists in her lap. The muscles in her jawline strained tightly. She was clearly upset about something.

When Carla began telling her story, she revealed a deep bitterness toward her father. She exclaimed, "He was an evil man and wicked! I hate him and hope he goes to hell and suffers for all the pain he caused me and the rest of our family."

If she had come to me for help some years ago, (back before I understood the things I do now,) I would certainly have empathized with her. Then I would have shown her the many Bible passages that instruct us concerning forgiveness, such as:

"... *as the Lord has forgiven you, so you also must forgive*" (implying that our forgiveness should be the same as the Lord's for us) Col. 3:13

*"... if you forgive others their trespasses, your heavenly Father will also forgive you"* (implying that if you don't forgive others, then He won't forgive you) Matt. 6:14

*"...judge not, and you will not be judged; condemn not, and you will not be condemned; forgive, and you will be forgiven"* (implying that if you don't forgive, then you will not be forgiven) Luke 6:37

*"Our Father in Heaven ... forgive us our debts, as we also have forgiven our debtors,"* (implying that God forgives us in the same measure that we forgive others) Matt. 6:12

### *Spiritual Persuasion and Coercion Applied as Needed*

After showing her the truth, I would have appealed to her conscience. I would have encouraged her to "do the right thing" and make the hard choice to forgive. Though at that time, I would not have admitted it, I was using these Bible passages as "spiritual pressure" to convince her to forgive even though she would have resisted such a notion.

At that time, I held the notion that if people were given the truth that they would be able to forgive. I believed that knowledge of the Bible produced spiritual outcomes. I believed that if Carla knew the truth about forgiveness, she could choose with her will to bring it about. Later we will see that this approach is the same approach used by the Children of Israel in their attempts to keep the Law. It did not work for them and it did not help Carla either. Just because she was given the truth, this did not mean that she could effectively do it.

My applying this "spiritual" persuasion and coercion would have probably resulted in her agreeing to forgive, or at least being willing to go through the motions. I would then have proceeded to lead her in a confessional prayer that would have come from me more than from her. It may have sounded something like this:

> *"I admit that I have bitterness and hatred toward my father, but today I choose to confess this as sin, and I repent and exercise my will to obey the Scriptures and willfully choose to forgive him for all he did. In Jesus' name, Amen."*

At this juncture, we would have assumed that the task was accomplished. She may even have experienced some sense of release and felt somewhat better. We would then have claimed the forgiveness to be effective, based upon her willful choice and obedience to the truth.

However, time will tell whether true forgiveness has occurred or not. If Carla had genuinely forgiven her father, her feelings of offense and resentment would lift off her permanently, and compassion would replace the hatred and bitterness she'd felt before. If the offense, anger, and resentment remained or later "came back," it is most likely that forgiveness did not occur.

If later, Carla had an encounter with her father after having *really* forgiven him for what he had done, then she will be able to stay in peace without being emotionally stirred up by his presence. If seeing him causes her to feel offended, angry, or irritated, etc., then it suggests there is something lacking in her forgiveness.

In all actuality, if the anger and resentment had resurfaced later, then it had never left in the first place. At best, the forgiveness was incomplete. We *cannot* forgive and then "un-forgive." However, it is possible to forgive a portion of the "debts" while retaining some unforgiveness of debts that have yet to be resolved. When this is the case, a portion of the anger, resentment, and hatred will also remain. We will learn more about this soon when we discuss the necessity of taking an account.

## *A Simple Test*

We will soon discover that forgiveness is dependent upon us knowing the truth with the heart and being able to view the person and debt from God's perspective. When we know the truth from God's perspective, we can view the person through the eyes of Christ. However, if an encounter with someone against whom we have harbored an offense continues to stir up troublesome emotions, this indicates that something remains unresolved. Genuine forgiveness releases us from the bitter and angry feelings we hold against those who have hurt us.

If Carla and I had wanted to check if forgiveness had occurred, I could simply have asked her, "When you think about all that your father did to you, what do you feel?" If she reported feeling completely peaceful and calm, with a sense of resolution and compassion toward him, then we might assume that something good had taken place. However, if my asking her how she felt toward her father resulted in her saying something like, "Not so good. I still feel angry and resentful toward him," then we could assume that something was amiss. When genuine forgiveness occurs, emotions will change in accordance with this reality. Later we will discover an important principle that states that emotion is an accurate indicator of what we believe.

Genuinely forgiving a person of his debt does not mean we will have a warm and friendly relationship with that person. That can only happen after a reconciliation has occurred in the relationship. Reconciliation is a different issue altogether from forgiveness. We will discuss this later.

> GENUINELY FORGIVING A PERSON OF HIS DEBT DOES NOT MEAN WE WILL HAVE A WARM AND FRIENDLY RELATIONSHIP WITH THAT PERSON. THAT CAN ONLY HAPPEN AFTER A RECONCILIATION HAS OCCURRED IN THE RELATIONSHIP. RECONCILIATION IS A DIFFERENT ISSUE ALTOGETHER FROM FORGIVENESS.

## *Defending the Territory*

According to my previous way of thinking, I would have told Carla not to trust her feelings, but to deny them and stand on the truth of her decision. I would have viewed forgiveness as territory that needed to be defended and a state that could be lost if not protected and maintained. If later, Carla should encounter her father and feel angry or resentful, I would have encouraged her to "stand her ground," deny what she was feeling, and claim by faith that she had forgiven. I might have even described her encounter as an attack from the devil and had her do some manner of spiritual warfare to defend her territory. Even though I was misinformed in doing some of these things, I was nonetheless, determined and committed to doing them.

At that time, I simply did not understand the purpose and value of a painful emotion. I viewed it as a bad thing and even as a "fiery arrow" shot our way by the devil to discourage us and defeat us. In general, I viewed negative emotion as something to be overcome. I had also mistakenly believed that we should not give attention to our emotions because they could not be trusted. My default plan of action was to deny what I felt and choose to do the truth. My motto was, "Obedience over pain!" "Trust and obey for there is no other way…" Although, this method never did work very well for me, I still prescribed it for others.

Back then, I would have affirmed Carla in her willingness to forgive and restated that maintaining her forgiveness is an act of the will based upon the truth. I would have told her to stand on the truth of the Scriptures and encouraged her to continue to choose to walk in that truth. I would have also warned her that the enemy would try to convince her to *re-engage her bitterness,* causing her to "un-forgive" her father. Even though doing this would have been ineffective and theologically impossible, it would still have been my course of action. To take all of these steps might seem lofty and noble, but this strategy is riddled with theological and practical difficulties.

The fact is, my strategy for forgiving simply did not work. This book is an attempt to offer what I believe to be a more biblical and effective way.

### *Painful emotion is like a good friend.*

A common belief is that our emotions cannot be trusted. This is simply not so. It is true that what we feel cannot be trusted to always tell us the truth, but emotion is very reliable and accurate in exposing what we believe, since we always feel whatever we believe. Although what we believe may or may not be the truth, discovering what we believe plays a vital role in true forgiveness. It is our lie-based beliefs that keep us stuck where we are and hinders our ability to genuinely forgive.

---

*IT IS TRUE THAT WHAT WE FEEL CANNOT BE TRUSTED TO ALWAYS TELL US THE TRUTH, BUT EMOTION IS VERY RELIABLE AND ACCURATE IN EXPOSING WHAT WE BELIEVE, SINCE WE ALWAYS FEEL WHATEVER WE BELIEVE.*

---

Painful emotion is like a good and reliable friend who is willing to point out our flaws that others are unwilling to tell us about. Emotion can be trusted to accurately expose what we believe with our hearts since we feel whatever we believe. If we reject and deny what we are feeling and do not attend to what our emotions reveal, we will remain in our deception. This would be much the same as ignoring that good friend and not paying any heed to what he or she has called to our attention.

If we will slow things down when we are struggling to forgive and examine carefully what we are feeling, we may discover that there is a negative emotion present. This emotion will probably be the very emotion which reflects the belief hindering us from forgiving. This belief will be supporting our "solution" to the problem that our forgiving might create. Most likely the emotion will be in the anger family: anger, wrath, bitterness, resentment, offense, rancor or hatred, etc.

Surprisingly, all negative emotions are beneficial when they are understood and used as God designed them to be used. For example, all our emotions are expressions of what we believe, and therefore, very beneficial in helping us to identify our heart belief. However, members of the anger family are unique from other lie-based emotions such as; fear, worry, anxiousness, or feeling helpless, powerless or out of control. We will discover later that emotions in the anger family are felt toward something or someone, where as other negative emotions are felt inwardly and not expressed outwardly. They are also intentional as they are serving a purpose, whereas other lie-based emotions are simply flowing from the belief they reflect.

---

*THOUGH WE MAY HAVE RIGHTFULLY FELT ANGER (OR ANY OTHER MEMBER OF THE ANGER FAMILY) WHEN THE PERSON DID SOMETHING (OR DIDN'T DO WHAT THEY SHOULD HAVE DONE), THE ANGER WE CONTINUE TO CARRY IS NO LONGER ABOUT THE TRUTH, BUT IS PERPETUALLY SUSTAINED BY A LIE.*

---

Though we may have rightfully felt anger (or any other member of the anger family) when the person did something (or didn't do what they should have done), the anger we continue to carry is no longer about the truth, but is perpetually sustained by a lie.

We will look at anger in detail in a later chapter, but suffice to say for now, anger is an expression of a belief and this belief will keep us from forgiving. We feel whatever we believe therefore, emotion can be our friend in helping us to identify the belief and better position ourselves to receive God's perspective.

### *Controlling emotions is futile.*

Therefore, we see a fundamental reason for us to explore what we are feeling in any given situation and especially when it comes to forgiveness. The emotion that is felt in these situations will accurately point to and expose what we believe is hindering our ability to forgive. In TPM we often say, "You feel whatever you believe." Emotion is a direct reflection of the belief from which it flows.

It is a mistake to think we can overcome, control or rise above these negative emotions. We cannot overcome them, defeat them, or even control them. We may suppress them, deny what we feel, and self-medicate to distract ourselves from them, but they will remain until the lie-based belief supporting them is replaced with the truth. Our emotions are not controlled by any of these strategies. The very fact that we have to do what we do indicates that we are being controlled by what we feel and not vice versa.

Someone might protest and say, "I don't let my emotions control me. I control them." This sounds noble, but the very fact that we give our emotions undue attention by trying to control and manage them reveals we are not actually in control of them. If our emotions demand our attention, then they are dictating what we do. Even if I am not acting out my anger, resentment, or wrath upon those around me, I will be acting them out in some other fashion.

> *The very fact that we give our emotions undue attention by trying to control and manage them reveals we are not actually in control of them. If our emotions demand our attention, then they are dictating what we do.*

### *Emotion Reveals a Deeper Issue*

All negative emotions are symptoms of a deeper issue: our wrong belief. Unless this belief is replaced by the Lord's perspective, we will have no other option but to continue to experience them because of that belief. The basic TPM principle that says, "we feel whatever we believe" is consistent and true.

Our anger, bitterness, and resentment - common barriers to forgiveness - are not enemies to defeat; they are indicators of a lie-based belief. We need not strive to overcome them. If we can actually *embrace* these feelings and allow them to point out the real problem (our belief), then we can move in the direction of forgiving from the heart. This a radically different approach from the usual formula, which I formerly practiced.

As bad as these emotions may feel, to reject or deny them is to cut ourselves off from the very means we have been given to identify the belief that is driving these emotions; the very thing that is hindering us from being able to forgive. Emotions are not something to deny or suppress, but as I said, to be regarded as trusted friends, pointing out to us that which needs our attention. Our negative emotions can point out the beliefs which are hindering us from letting go of the offenses we are tightly clutching that are making us unable to forgive from the heart. Until we are able to identify the reason (belief) that we are unwilling to forgive and receive God's perspective, no measure of strong determination or willpower will loosen our clutches. However, when we know the truth in our hearts and can view the offending person and his offense through the lens of truth, forgiveness can follow without effort.

### *Forgiveness requires more than an act of the will.*

The idea that forgiveness is an act of the will coupled with obedience to the truth suggests it can be achieved through willpower and determination. During the years I tried to lead people into forgiveness using this approach, the success rate was anything but encouraging. I now realize that *forgiveness from the heart is not about willpower, determination, or even obedience.* Rather, *forgiveness is the natural outcome of our own freedom that comes from knowing the truth with our heart.* Another way of saying this might be, forgiveness is not something that we do, but a natural and expected outcome of what we have been given.

When the Spirit persuades us of His truth, the lie-based beliefs that kept us from forgiving will be cast out and replaced with His perspective. When His light of truth shines in our hearts, we will release the debts of those who have hurt us without effort.

---

*FORGIVENESS FROM THE HEART IS NOT ABOUT WILLPOWER, DETERMINATION, OR EVEN OBEDIENCE. RATHER, FORGIVENESS IS THE NATURAL OUTCOME OF OUR OWN FREEDOM THAT COMES FROM KNOWING THE TRUTH WITH OUR HEART... FORGIVENESS IS NOT SOMETHING THAT WE DO, BUT A NATURAL AND EXPECTED OUTCOME OF WHAT WE HAVE BEEN GIVEN.*

---

We find lasting freedom when we view the person and the debts from God's perspective, through heart-felt belief. God accomplishes this in us in the same manner that He demonstrates the fruits of the Spirit through us: He brings it about by the supernatural work of the Spirit. It is not something we can accomplish on our own.

Forgiveness is not an act of the will accomplished by strong determination or willpower, but rather the expected outcome of believing the truth with the heart. Jesus taught His disciples to forgive from the heart. However, heart belief is not something that we just decide to have, but is only bestowed upon us by the Spirit as He persuades us of His truth.

We cannot "do the fruit," but we can bear it. In similar fashion, we cannot "do forgiveness," but when the Spirit releases us from our own lie-based bondage, we are free to release others from the debts they owe us.

### *Choosing to forgive with our will is like trying to keep the Law.*

Most believers know that forgiving those who have wronged them is the right thing to do and the biblical expectation. However, trying to simply obey the truth we know rarely produces a long-term solution. Nonetheless, it is the means commonly advocated for living the Christian life. This is the same approach that the Children of Israel took towards the Law. This has never worked and will not work when applied to forgiveness. When we approach forgiveness with a "thou shalt forgive or you won't be forgiven" understanding, then forgiveness will remain elusive.

Unfortunately, this strategy is encouraged repeatedly, from pulpits all around the world. The message goes something like this, "The Bible says this _____ [the particular truth], so stop doing what you are doing [the sinful behavior] and choose to start doing what the Bible says." This message creates a predictable cycle of defeat for the believer, since it is the same strategy practiced in all other world religions. *It focuses upon endeavoring to conform our behavior to the truth, as opposed to our being transformed by the truth.*

The New Testament makes it clear that we are no longer under the Law, but under grace. We are not called or expected to produce good works of ourselves, because good works are an outcome of the indwelling Christ (Gal. 2:20). The fruit of the Spirit, good works, and forgiveness are all brought forth by and from the same source: The Spirit. All are the outcome of Christ living in us and are not achieved through self-effort. We are *fruit bearers* and not *fruit producers. Forgiveness is a fruit that God can bring about within us, but not something we can do ourselves.*

Genuine forgiveness flows effortlessly from believing the truth that the Spirit has deposited within our hearts. It goes far beyond what we may intellectually believe. Choosing to forgive someone because we know it is the right thing to do rarely works. If we could do this, then the means for forgiving would be to push through the contrary emotions, choose to obey, and just forgive. Realistically, it is unlikely that genuine forgiveness will occur simply because we choose to do it, even if it is an act of obedience to what we believe to be the truth.

---

*FORGIVENESS IS A FRUIT THAT GOD CAN BRING ABOUT WITHIN US, BUT NOT SOMETHING WE CAN DO OURSELVES.*

---

Those who have been "obedient" and have "chosen to forgive" may indeed experience a lull in their inner storm of resentment, however, time will tell whether genuine forgiveness has occurred or not. If they are required to relate to those they presume they have forgiven and the storm clouds re-appear with a torrent of resentment flooding back in, then forgiveness has not yet come about. It is common to demonstrate outward compliance and a harmonious attitude, while inwardly struggling with recurring antagonism.

## *Unfortunate Default Plan of Action: If at first you don't succeed, try harder*

If forgiving by willful obedience is our plan of action, yet the choice to forgive fails to bring about genuine and lasting freedom (which is common), then our only resort is to try harder. "Trying harder" is usually the default method for maturing in the Christian life, but the success rate is dismal. We try hard to obey God's Word and to do the right thing by asking ourselves, "What would Jesus do?" We strive to carry out the fruit of the Spirit as a task to perform, but the ultimate outcome of even the best endeavor is exhaustion and eventual failure. *God has not called us to perform to become like Jesus, but rather He has called us to enter into what already is: the finished work of Christ.* This finished work makes us like Him apart from our own efforts by transforming us into His image. He has called us to cease from our labor and enter into the finished work of His rest (Heb. 4:9-10).

If we are born again we *are* children of God. He did not birth children that "look" like anyone other than Himself. Jesus was the firstborn, and many are born again after Him, just as the Scriptures declare, *"... He would be the firstborn among many brethren..."* (Rom. 8:29). *The Christian life is not a journey of becoming like Jesus, but rather it is a journey of discovering what transpired the moment we believed and learning to walk in that present reality.* We are not called to try and act like or look like Jesus, but we are called to walk in the Spirit of Truth and to allow His Spirit to transform us.

---

*God has not called us to perform in order to become like Jesus, but rather He has called us to enter into what already is: the finished work of Christ. This finished work makes us like Him apart from our own efforts by transforming us into His image. He has called us to cease from our labor and enter into the finished work of His rest (Heb. 4:9-10).*

---

Rather than trying harder to forgive, we need to go deeper and discover the reason why forgiving, in many situations, is so difficult. As we have seen, when it is difficult to forgive, it is often because we are harboring lie-based beliefs which prevent forgiveness from being truly released. But when the Spirit persuades our hearts of the truth, we will forgive without effort. This is the expected and natural outcome of Christ living His life in and through us. *"...it is no longer I who live but Christ..."* (Gal. 2:20).

## *The Reality of Effortless Forgiveness*

If we limit ourselves to a mere intellectual belief of what the Bible says concerning forgiveness, without letting it touch our hearts, its challenge will overwhelm us. It will force us to deny what we feel and try to obey what it says through sheer effort and willpower. Here again, like the children of Israel trying to keep the Law, defeat is very predictable. When what we believe with our hearts conflicts with our intellectual belief, a struggle ensues. Therefore, forgiveness can be so elusive, difficult, and unattainable. We can know the truth intellectually, desire to do it, and even go through all the motions, but until the truth is believed with the heart, forgiveness is highly improbable.

---

*THE CHRISTIAN LIFE IS NOT A JOURNEY OF BECOMING LIKE JESUS, BUT RATHER IT IS A JOURNEY OF DISCOVERING WHAT TRANSPIRED THE MOMENT WE BELIEVED AND LEARNING TO WALK IN THAT PRESENT REALITY. WE ARE NOT CALLED TO TRY AND ACT LIKE OR LOOK LIKE JESUS, BUT WE ARE CALLED TO WALK IN THE SPIRIT OF TRUTH AND TO ALLOW HIS SPIRIT TO TRANSFORM US.*

---

We are told to forgive one another in the same way that Christ has forgiven us (Eph. 4:32). However, as we examine the forgiveness the Lord brings, there appears to be no indication that He had to work at it. Without question, His forgiveness cost Him much, but His choice to forgive was an easy decision for Him. As a matter of fact, it was because of the "... *joy set before Him...*" (Heb. 12:2) that Jesus endured the cross and freely gave us this great gift. His forgiveness flowed effortlessly from the truth and from His heart of love. We are called to do the same. One of the purposes of this book is to explain why it is so hard to forgive and to provide a way for forgiveness to become effortless.

We will soon look behind the curtain to discover what hinders us from forgiving as the Lord forgave. Our unwillingness to forgive probably isn't because we lack sincerity of heart or a desire to do what is right. However, even when we genuinely try our best to forgive, the success rate is still very low. I want to suggest that the reason for this inability to forgive is not really complicated. It rests solely upon one thing: our belief.

*What follows is a list of discussion questions. More questions like these will follow each chapter. They are designed to remind you of what you have learned and to open up discussion if you are part of a group. Use them as seems best for you and your setting. If you are studying this book as a part of a small group, do not let the discussion questions dictate what you do, but let them help facilitate what you are doing.*

# *Discussion Questions*

1. What has been your experience with forgiving those who have hurt you? Success stories? Failures?

2. How did you know whether genuine forgiveness had occurred or not? What were the indicators?

3. What is your initial reaction to the idea that we feel whatever we believe and that our emotions expose what we really believe? For example, how can we say that we believe the Bib*le verse, "God will supply all of your needs according to His riches in* glory…" (Phil. 4:19) and yet still worry over our finances?

4. If our negative emotion is indeed our "friend" pointing out what we believe, how might this change how we live our daily lives? How might it impact how we relate to those around us?

5. How do you react to the idea that whatever we believe in our hearts will either allow us to forgive or keep us enmeshed with those with whom we are embittered?

6. How do you react to the idea that genuine *forgiveness* flows effortlessly from believing the truth with the heart?

7. The common strategy to live the Christian life within the *church community* is trying harder. What are some of the fundamental problems with this approach? What is the implied premise of such a strategy?

8. We are told in the Scriptures to forgive one another in the same way that Christ has forgiven us (Eph. 4:32). How much effort did Jesus put into forgiving us? What does this say about how we are to forgive?

# Chapter One

## What is Transformation Prayer Ministry

This book is about the principles of forgiveness. However, many of the principles that will be shared are borrowed from a ministry model that I (Ed Smith) developed some years ago that we call Transformation Prayer Ministry (TPM). Pastors, mental health professionals, lay ministers as well as lay people are practicing the principles of TPM in over 200 countries worldwide with a reported great success. The ministry began in 1995 in my small town Christian family counseling practice where I initially gave the process the name Theophostic Prayer Ministry. *Theos* is New Testament Greek for God and *Phos* is the Greek word for light. Therefore, we have "God's Light/Theophostic."

The focus of the ministry during the early years of its development was upon helping emotionally troubled people to identify their lie-based heart beliefs and helping them to position themselves before God to receive His perspective resulting in genuine and lasting freedom. Today the focus has shifted from just helping the emotionally wounded to helping all members of the Body of Christ who want to participate with God as He refines their faith, renews their minds and transforms their lives. TPM is an effective way to do this.

The purpose of this book is not to train you in this ministry model, but to present some of the basic concepts and principles taught within it as they relate to forgiveness. It will benefit you to have at least the working understanding of TPM that we will provide shortly. You may obtain a fuller understanding of TPM from the TPM website where all the training is made freely available. See *www.transformationprayer.org*

**From burnout a ministry is born.**

Over twenty years ago I (Ed Smith) reached a point of frustration and burnout in my pastoral counseling ministry. The focus of my work at that time was on helping people—primarily women—who reported having been sexually abused as children. Many of these women came for help with additional issues such as eating disorders, sexual dysfunctions, panic disorders, anxiety, addictions, and depression. These women had legitimate reason to be angry, having been violated and abused by perpetrators of evil. Needless to say, forgiveness was not something that initially interested them.

I spent over five years trying to help them find freedom, but eventually became burned out in defeat and discouragement. This happened because I didn't see any real and lasting change, even after years of working with them. With my help, they had become successful managers of their pain but did not show signs of any real freedom. The possibility of forgiveness was rarely considered, although I often encouraged them to do this.

However, it was in this place of personal discouragement that I had the glorious privilege of witnessing God do what only He can do. His intervention of truth resulted in many of these women finding freedom from the lies that had held them captive all their lives. It was in this context, one I had deemed hopeless, that the ministry we now call Transformation Prayer was born.

### *Wearing the right glasses makes all the difference.*

Our lie-based beliefs are like eye glasses through which we view and interpret life. Once we put them on, it is impossible to view life in any other way. They become the lenses through which we view all subsequent life experiences which are similar. Therefore, our adult relationships feel strangely familiar, reflecting those we experienced in childhood. This causes us to say things like, "You are just like my father," "You are just like my mother," and other similar statements. Our present situations look and feel the same as those we have been in before.

Sometimes we try to wear two pairs of glasses at the same time. We may intellectually believe a particular biblical truth with our minds, yet believe something completely contrary to this truth with our hearts. For example, we may believe the Bible verse that says God will supply all of our needs (Phil 4:19), and yet live in worry and fear over our finances. This indicates that although we know what the Bible says with our intellect, our emotions are exposing what we believe with our hearts.

The problem is with our "glasses". Our vision becomes completely distorted because of the lens prescriptions of our heart belief and intellectual belief are not the same. James the Apostle calls this being "double minded." It means that we are holding two or more opposing beliefs at the same time: one with the intellect and the other with the heart.

It is possible (and very common) to believe the truth with our intellect while harboring an opposing belief in our hearts. However, we cannot hold two opposing heart beliefs at the same time or two opposing intellectual beliefs at the same time. I cannot believe intellectually that 2+2=4 and believe 2+2=6 at the same time. Neither can I believe with my heart that God loves and accepts me and concurrently believe He hates and rejects me. However, we can believe something with our intellect and believe the opposite with our hearts.

If I believe God is my protector and still live in fear, or that God is my provider and continue to worry about how I will pay the bills, this indicates that I have heart beliefs and intellectual beliefs which oppose each other.

---

*DOUBLE-MINDEDNESS: HOLDING TWO OR MORE OPPOSING BELIEFS AT THE SAME TIME. WHEN WHAT WE BELIEVE WITH THE HEART IS CONTRARY TO WHAT WE BELIEVE WITH OUR INTELLECT. AS LONG AS WE BELIEVE LIES IN OUR HEARTS THAT ARE CONTRARY TO THE TRUTH TO WHICH WE GIVE INTELLECTUAL ASSENT, GENUINE FORGIVENESS WILL BE ELUSIVE.*

---

We can hold the intellectual belief that God loves us and even quote the supporting Scriptures, while still feeling unloved, rejected, and abandoned because of contrary beliefs we hold in our hearts. It is common for people to know the truth intellectually and yet have a contrary heart belief. Because this is true, even though we intellectually believe that the Bible calls us to forgive our debtors, doing so remains a struggle. As long as we believe lies in our hearts that contradict the truth we believe in our minds, genuine forgiveness remains elusive.

### *Current belief is the lens of interpretation.*

For the women whom I tried to help in my early years of ministry, it was their current beliefs and not their memories that provided the "lenses" through which they viewed their past and interpreted their present. The emotional pain they currently felt was not because of what had happened to them. It was because of what they *still* believed.

These women knew logically and intellectually that they were no longer in danger, that the abuse they had suffered was not their fault, that it did not make them dirty or shameful, and that they were not powerless today—even though they did not have control as children. Nevertheless, their lie-based heart beliefs still felt true, causing them to feel painful emotions.

Herein lies the problem: heart belief always overrides intellectual belief, even when we know that the heart belief is a lie. This is why these women would often say such things as, "I know it's not true, but it still feels true," "I know I was innocent, but I still feel shameful," or "I know I am safe now, but I still feel afraid."

### *Heart belief always feels true.*

One characteristic of heart belief is that it always feels true even when it is not. Unfortunately, much of what we believe intellectually about the Bible does not feel true nor does it produce any emotion at all. Indeed, it is often accompanied by some measure of doubting. The next time you are reading from the Bible, ask yourself, "Does what I am reading *feel* absolutely true?" (Not *is* it true, but does it *feel* true.) If it doesn't feel true, then why doesn't it? If we believe it, then it should feel true.

If someone tells you something and it does not feel true to you, do you believe them anyway? Probably not. If what we say we believe does not feel true, then we do not believe it with our hearts, even though we may agree with it intellectually.

We may believe the Bible intellectually and even be willing to give up our lives for matters to which we give intellectual assent. However, if it does not feel true, then it is not our heart belief. It remains merely intellectual assent. Again, I remind you that even though we say we believe the Bible verse that says God will supply all of our needs (Phil 4:19), (and yet) ever feel worried, anxious, or fearful concerning our finances, then we do not believe it with our hearts. If we believe this verse with our hearts, it is impossible to feel fearful, anxious, or worried over our money matters. Or if we say we believe that God is in control of our lives, our protector who is watching out for us, and yet live in fear, then we do not believe He is what we say we believe He is. Our emotions always expose what we believe in our hearts.

### *Emotional pain was not caused by the abuse.*

After many years of working with these women, I came to realize that their present emotional pain was NOT due to their abuse, but to what they had come to believe and continued to believe as true in the context of their abuse. Their current lie-based belief was the outcome of their initial interpretation of their abuse that had followed them throughout their lives. It was not what they used to believe that was affecting them, but what they continued to believe - the belief that had followed them into the present. Neither was the memory of the event at the root of their problem. It was not what happened to them years before that caused them to feel badly today, but what they currently believed. They did not have painful memories, but rather painful beliefs that remembering the abuse triggered within them.

As strange as it may seem, it is not the memory of what happens to us that causes us to feel what we feel, but rather the belief we developed at that time and still currently believe. The reason that their memories of the abuse still stung these women was because of what they continued to believe about it, not because of what happened. Their belief was the problem. If the memory had indeed been the reason for their pain, then there would be no hope for freedom, for the past cannot be changed. (We will discuss the importance of memory in forgiving in a later chapter.)

Beliefs such as, "It was my fault," "I should have stopped it," "I am dirty and shameful," "I am out of control," "I am going to die," "There is something wrong with me," (and many others) were the roots of their current emotional pain.

***If the past was the problem, then there would be no present solution.***

If it were true that our past is the root of our current problem, then there would be no remedy, since the past cannot be changed. However, if our current problem is, in fact, rooted in what we currently believe, albeit learned during an earlier life experience, then this can be changed. Yet changing our lie-based heart belief is not possible by sheer willpower or self-determination. Nor can it be changed simply because someone, such as a counselor, provides us with truth.

In the early years of my ministry (Ed), I witnessed many people struggling to forgive; even though, when I pointed it out to them, they agreed intellectually with what the Bible said concerning the issue. I led them to confess their "sins," repent, and choose by an act of their will to forgive. Many applied themselves with all diligence, but as long as their heart belief remained contrary to the truth, they were unable to truly forgive. Unless our intellectual understanding and belief about forgiving can be brought into line with God's perspective within our hearts, forgiveness cannot follow.

I tried to help Carla, as well as the other women, realize the truth. I did the obvious: I told them the truth—over and over. I had them memorize Bible verses. I had them journal the truth. I encouraged them to deny the pain, believe the truth, and stand on it—name it and claim it. Nevertheless, despite doing all of the above, the pain was still present when they recalled the memory.

I encouraged them again and again to "put their past behind them," only to discover that doing so was an impossible task. I now realize that attempting to put the past behind us is nothing more than "spiritualized" suppression. Suppression is not a good thing, and it brings no benefits. It has never solved the assumed "pain problem" and only creates new problems of its own. Choosing to not think about the past will have no impact on the lies we learned in our past, and continue to believe.

---

*Choosing to not think about the past will have no impact on the lies we learned in our past, and continue to believe.*

---

The idea of putting our past behind us comes from a misinterpretation of Philippians 3:13, where the Apostle Paul spoke of putting his efforts in self-righteousness behind him. This we must do. However, putting our memories behind us is impossible and has no benefit. Our memories are not a source of trouble. Our troubles all spring from what we believe.

The truth is, the past was not the problem for these women. The problem was the belief that they had brought forward and still currently believed. Even more importantly, their current lie-based belief—which they had learned in their childhood— was greatly impacting their present life in a variety of destructive ways.

### Even though they knew the truth, they were not free.

What had me so perplexed was that they knew the truth logically and rationally. They intellectually knew that the abuse they suffered was not their fault, they were not dirty or shameful, and that they were safe now and no longer in danger. Nonetheless, when they revisited the abuse memory they still *felt* trapped, dirty, out of control, shameful, small, and helpless.

It was amazing to watch them counsel each other during a support group meeting. One would be agonizing in her pain as she walked through a memory, while another one would be telling her the truth. "You are not there anymore! You are safe now. It was not your fault." Then when the same one who had given counsel would work through her own memory, she would cry out in similar pain, "I'm trapped, dirty, and I'm going to die!" They each knew the truth with their minds, but their hearts still ruled their emotions.

Even though they knew the truth intellectually, their lie-based heart beliefs still felt true; their heart belief trumped what they knew with their rational minds. In Transformation Prayer Ministry, we often use the phrase, "We feel whatever we believe." Whatever I believe with my heart will produce what I feel in any given moment.

This is where life can become very frustrating. I can know intellectually that God is my provider and yet live in a constant state of worry and fear over my finances. My emotions are always a dead giveaway of what I believe, even when I can quote the Bible verse that states otherwise. What was true for these women—that they were safe, not being hurt, not dirty or shameful, etc. — simply did not feel true because they believed something else with their hearts.

I was in a quandary as to what to do to help them. Telling them the truth was not working. However, it was in this context that Transformation Prayer Ministry was born.

### Breakthrough: "What does the Lord want you to know?"

One day in a ministry session I asked one of the women if she would be willing to try something different from what we had been doing. She agreed. I asked her to think about one of her abuse memories and tell me what she felt. She almost immediately began to cry and tremble as she described feeling shame, fear, and guilt. I asked her why she felt that way. She told me her belief, "I know this is not true, but it feels like what happened was my fault and because of what happened I am dirty and shameful."

Here is where I would have typically told her the truth. Instead, I took a deep breath and prayed out loud, "Jesus, I do not know what to do. Is there something that You want her to know?" I honestly did not have any expectations about what might happen. I had simply run out of options. After a few moments, she stopped crying and calmed down. She sat up and opened her eyes and with a bewildered, yet very peaceful look, she said, "It's gone." I said, "What's gone?" She said, "The shame and guilt all lifted off me." I asked, "How is that?" She replied with a countenance of joy, "He said I'm not there anymore and it was not my fault." I responded, "I know, that's what I told you." She said, "Yes, but this time, HE told me." I said with some hesitation, "Who?" She said, "The Lord told me that it was not my fault!"

### *Heart belief was the missing key.*

The missing key is the fact that *only* God can speak truth to our hearts. Believing with the heart is an outcome of the Spirit persuading us of the truth. These women needed to know the truth in their hearts that they already knew with their minds. I had already told them the truth over and again, my mind to their minds, but I had not been able to communicate this truth to their hearts. Although there is value in knowing the truth intellectually, only heart belief can free us to walk in the effortless victory God desires for us. Victory that requires effort or contains some element of struggle is not true victory. Victory is only realized when the battle is over, and the flag has been raised. This is the victory that God has for us.

---

*VICTORY THAT REQUIRES EFFORT OR CONTAINS SOME ELEMENT OF STRUGGLE IS NOT TRUE VICTORY. VICTORY IS ONLY REALIZED WHEN THE BATTLE IS OVER, AND THE FLAG HAS BEEN RAISED. THIS IS THE VICTORY THAT GOD HAS FOR US.*

---

### *A purified heart belief is the essence of faith and our only pathway to freedom and victory.*

Heart belief is the essence of faith—knowing the truth with our heart with absolute certainty. Only God can grant us faith by persuading us of the truth in our hearts. It was by faith we entered into salvation and it is by faith we continue the journey, for "*...as you have received Christ Jesus the Lord, so walk in Him*" (Col. 2:6). True victory (absence of struggle and battle) is only achieved through faith, as it says, "*...this is the victory that has overcome the world—our faith*" (1 Jo. 5:4).

---

*HEART BELIEF IS THE ESSENCE OF FAITH—KNOWING THE TRUTH WITH OUR HEART WITH ABSOLUTE CERTAINTY.*

---

Since that first "TPM" ministry session— now over two decades ago— and after many thousands of hours of applying this prayer model of ministry, we have developed a clearly defined and systematic process to facilitate transformation. This process is very consistent because it relies on the way God designed our minds to work. It is totally dependent upon His faithfulness, as we learn to work in harmony with what He has been doing all along.

TPM is not something new or something created. God has been doing this very thing all along. We simply happened to recognize what was occurring and developed a system by which we can intentionally cooperate with God as He refines our faith, renews our minds, and transforms our lives.

TPM does not attempt to replace anything the church may provide to teach, instruct, counsel or encourage its members in living the Christian life and coming into full maturity in the knowledge of Christ (Eph. 4:13). TPM simply offers a means by which each member can intentionally cooperate with what God is doing in refining their faith, renewing their minds and transforming their lives, by positioning themselves to receive His truth.

### *Our belief hinders forgiveness.*

So, what does all of this have to do with forgiveness? Again, forgiveness from the heart cannot occur apart from knowing the truth with the heart, and only God can bring that about. Knowing the truth intellectually is something that any person can accomplish if they set their mind to doing it. Even an unbeliever can gain intellectual knowledge in the Scriptures. However, only God can persuade us of the truth within our hearts. It is from the heart that genuine forgiveness occurs. Unlike the unsuccessful process I was pursuing with Carla and so many others, genuine forgiveness through heart belief is a work of God.

I can inform people of the truth by reading them the appropriate Bible verses, and follow by encouraging them to confess their sins, turn to God, and choose forgiveness. However, if their lie-based heart belief does not change, it will keep them from forgiving. When Carla and others agreed with me to do these former things, they became saddled with the task of maintaining a "forgiveness" that had never occurred. This did not bring relief, but was an added burden to a heart already weighed down with unforgiveness.

If I had asked these women how they felt about forgiving their abusers when they first came to me for help, none would have even considered the possibility of being able to do this, even though they possessed the intellectual knowledge that forgiveness was necessary and would be beneficial. Without exception, each one would have felt strong resistance and hesitation at the thought of forgiving her abuser.

Each of these women also harbored deep emotional pain that was produced by the lie-based heart beliefs learned at the time of their abuse. Each felt emotions such as shame, fear, worry, panic, and a feeling of being out of control. These particular negative emotions were caused by lie-based heart beliefs such as "I am dirty because of what happened to me," "What happened was my fault," "I am trapped and out of control," "I am worthless," and "God has abandoned me." Each believed she was tainted, unlovable, worthless, and abandoned. These heart beliefs needed to be resolved with the truth before forgiveness could occur.

### *Belief that Supports a Solution*

The emotions just mentioned (shame, fear, guilt, being out of control, feeling helpless and powerless, among others) all flow from lies believed with the heart. These lies are established through the interpretation we give to life events and become our current lie-based beliefs. These lies must be resolved before effectual forgiveness can occur.

Along with these women's lie-based heart beliefs came additional lie-based beliefs that provided them with logical and rational reasons for holding on to their debts. These additional lies generally produce emotions very different from those produced by heart beliefs. Whereas heart belief emotions are felt inwardly, these emotions are felt *toward* those who had caused the hurt. Emotions such as anger, rage, hate, bitterness, resentment, rancor, and hostility, are all felt *toward* someone or something. Emotions produced by heart belief, such as fear, worry, anxiety, hopelessness, and helplessness, are all felt inwardly.

There is an important distinction here. Lie-based heart belief is the outcome of our faulty interpretation of our life situation. This lie-based heart belief produces emotions such as fear, worry, anxiety, hopelessness, helplessness, etc. These emotions are rooted in either what we believe about ourselves (self-identity) or what we believe about our situation (state of being). However, the belief behind anger, resentment, rancor, hate rage, etc. is of a different kind.

It was these other lies (not heart belief) that were keeping the women from being able to let go of the debt, and forgive from their hearts. Nonetheless, the heart belief also needed to be changed before forgiveness could be accomplished. Both types of lies need to be addressed.

### *Solutions that Do Not Work*

This second type of lie provided *a solution* for a perceived problem. In TPM we call this type of belief a *"solution belief."* There are many different forms in which a solution belief can manifest itself in a person's life. In this book we are focused primarily on beliefs that are related to holding onto the debt and our unwillingness to forgive.

*Solution beliefs* are designed to protect us from perceived harm, maintain our sense of control, hold people accountable, and so on. In the context of an unwillingness to forgive, there will always be a solution belief present. The withholding of forgiveness is motivated by a belief that this will solve a perceived problem that would otherwise go unresolved. It is believed that if forgiveness is offered, then an unacceptable problem would remain for us.

For example, one might reason something along these lines: "If I forgive, I will get hurt again (the problem needing to be solved), so not forgiving keeps me safe (the belief)." Or, "If I forgive my abuser, he will get away with what he did (the problem needing to be solved), so not forgiving holds him accountable and punishes him (the belief)." Or, "If I forgive, I will lose control (the problem needing to be solved), so by not forgiving I maintain some measure of control (the belief)."

These lies are all a form of protection, control, or a solution to a perceived problem. We will look at this idea later in this book when we discuss what we call "Solution Beliefs" in TPM. We will discover that before a person can forgive from his heart, he must be free of the solution beliefs that are causing him to resist forgiving. He also must know the truth where his heart belief has been contrary to it. When the Spirit persuades us of the truth within our hearts and displaces the beliefs we have established to solve our perceived problems, forgiveness will be the expected outcome. This forgiveness will flow *effortlessly* from the truth we know within our hearts.

---

> **WHEN THE SPIRIT PERSUADES US OF THE TRUTH WITHIN OUR HEARTS AND DISPLACES THE BELIEFS WE HAVE ESTABLISHED TO SOLVE OUR PERCEIVED PROBLEMS, FORGIVENESS WILL BE THE EXPECTED OUTCOME.**

---

Only forgiveness that comes from the heart is lasting and an expression of our own freedom. Jesus understood this when He instructed His disciples to forgive from their hearts (Matt. 18:35). This book will continue to explore heart belief and how to forgive from the heart.

## *Discussion Questions*

1. What do you do if you remember something that feels painful?

2. If the painful feelings we feel when we remember a particular memory is not coming from the memory, but rather the belief we currently believe, why might remembering be a good thing?

3. Why might the old saying, "forgive and forget" lack credence and be something we cannot do?

4. How do the "glasses" that we wear impact our current relationships? Why might our current relationships sometimes feel like those of our childhood?

5. What is the fundamental flaw in trying to put our past behind us? How is trying to do so a form of "spiritualized" suppression? How might suppressing our past prove detrimental as opposed to being a solution to our issues?

6. What is the difference between believing the truth with our intellect and believing it with our hearts? Why do you think heart belief overrides intellectual belief in any real-life situation?

7. What are examples of believing the truth with your mind, but believing something contrary with your heart?

8. Why do you think it requires the Spirit to persuade us to believe the truth with the heart as opposed to our just choosing to believe?

9. In what ways have you made the connection between heart belief and forgiveness? Why is forgiveness not possible until we know the truth in our hearts?

# Chapter Two

## Forgiving from the Heart

*Forgiveness is an expected outcome of being persuaded of God's truth in the heart.*

Jesus instructed His disciples to "...forgive from the heart..." (Matt. 18:35). Heart forgiveness flows from the truth we believe with our hearts. It is only because God has persuaded us of His truth within our hearts that we can forgive.

Genuine forgiveness flows effortlessly from knowing the truth with the heart. When we are able to view others and their offenses from God's perspective, we will be able to forgive them without effort as a natural outcome of our faith. Jesus looked out over the angry crowd who had nailed him to the cross and asked the Father to forgive them. How could He do this? Because of His heart belief. He knew the truth. We each need heart belief in the truth so that we too can forgive. The Bible gives us clear instruction as to how we are to forgive: "...just as the Lord forgave you, so also should you" (Col. 3:13). Jesus forgave from His heart because He knew the truth. This is how we are to forgive as well.

> *GENUINE FORGIVENESS FLOWS EFFORTLESSLY FROM KNOWING THE TRUTH WITH THE HEART. WHEN WE ARE ABLE TO VIEW OTHERS AND THEIR OFFENSES FROM GOD'S PERSPECTIVE, WE WILL BE ABLE TO FORGIVE THEM WITHOUT EFFORT AS A NATURAL OUTCOME OF OUR FAITH.*

### *Understanding Heart Belief*

Genuine forgiveness cannot occur unless it flows from truth that is believed with the heart. The Bible refers to the idea of heart belief in many places, drawing a distinction between what we believe with our hearts and what we believe with our intellect. It is "... with the heart a person believes, resulting in righteousness, and with the mouth he confesses, resulting in salvation" (Rom. 10:10). In contrast, believing the Gospel with the intellect provides no guarantee of salvation. Even the "demons also believe, and shudder" (Ja. 2:19), but they are not changed by the truth.

We will shortly discover why heart belief is necessary to fully understand and apply the principles of forgiveness. Too often people try to forgive their offenders by deliberate choice, based upon their intellectual understanding of what the Bible teaches about forgiveness. Forgiveness flows from the heart, not from ardent determination. Forgiveness is an expression of faith (knowing the truth with the heart). Willfully choosing to obey the truth and walking effortlessly in faith are two very different things.

### *Heart Belief Surpasses Knowledge.*

The Apostle Paul again reveals this distinction when he encourages us to "... know the love of Christ which surpasses knowledge, that you may be filled up to all the fullness of God" (Eph. 3:19). This passage reveals several things.

First, there is a knowing of something that supersedes our intellect. This is a realm of knowing provided for the believer in order that he might be filled up with the fullness of God. This is belief of the heart. I don't know the full meaning of "the fullness of God," but it sounds glorious!

We do know that it is heart belief which results in our righteous position in Christ; "... with the heart a person believes, resulting in righteousness..." (Rom. 10:10). We also know that we are called to walk out our faith in the same way we entered into our salvation; "... as you have received Christ Jesus the Lord, so walk in Him..." (Col. 2:6).

---

*When we are able to view others and their offenses from God's perspective, we will be able to forgive them without effort as a natural outcome of our faith.*

---

### *Because We Possess, We Do*

In the context of TPM, we equate heart belief with faith. We do not use the word faith to describe something that we do—but rather as something that we possess. It is because we possess faith, that we do what we do. It is because God has persuaded us of the truth that we believe and therefore, trust. It is because God has persuaded us of the truth in our hearts (faith) that we do good works and naturally experience the fruit of the Spirit. Everything begins with God and is continued by God and is also completed by Him. As the Apostle Paul declared, "...I am confident of this very thing, that He who began a good work in you will perfect it until the day of Christ Jesus" (Phil. 1:6) The work described here is what God is doing and will do and not a partnership with us. There is something that we must do, but it is not included in this passage. There is a necessity that must be fulfilled in us, but again it is what God must do. We are merely the ones receiving the provision.

Therefore, we must first be "...filled with the knowledge of His will in all spiritual wisdom and understanding, SO THAT [we] will walk in a manner worthy of the Lord, to please Him in all respects, bearing fruit in every good work and increasing in the knowledge of God" (Col. 1:9-10).

Jesus was asked one day by the same group of people He had fed the loaves and fishes, "What shall we do, so that we may work the works of God?" This group was looking for the behavior they needed to perform. Jesus answered with complete clarity when He said, "This is the work of God, that you believe in Him Whom He has sent." The same remains true for us today. The work we do is to believe. Belief from the heart will produce the behavior. When we are filled "with the knowledge of Him in all spiritual wisdom and understanding" (that only He can bring about), the works will follow.

### *A Divine Order of Things*

Did you notice the "so that" in the very middle of this passage? The "so that" reveals a divine order of things; one thing must be in place before the other can occur. Before we can do something, we must possess something. We can only walk worthy of the Lord, please Him, bear fruit and grow in knowledge of God after He has granted us the "knowledge of His will in all spiritual wisdom and understanding." This becomes heart belief, or faith. First He grants, then we possess, and then we do.

Not only do we possess faith, but this heart belief goes far beyond our adjustable intellectual belief. Faith, or heart belief, remains static. There is no wavering in faith that God gives or in what He has bestowed upon us. The gift and the giver are steadfast and sure as "... every good thing given and every perfect gift is from above, coming down from the Father of lights, with whom there is no variation or shifting shadow" (Ja. 1:17).

The writer of Hebrews broadens our understanding of faith by defining it as the "...assurance of things hoped for and the conviction of things not seen" (Heb. 11:1). Faith is knowing something with an absolute certainty, born of assurance and conviction. In TPM we define faith as the "Spirit's persuasion of the truth that we believe in our hearts, with an absolute certainty." Faith that is produced by the Spirit's persuasion is pure "...without any doubting" (Ja. 1:6).

---

*BEFORE WE CAN DO SOMETHING, WE MUST POSSESS SOMETHING. WE CAN ONLY WALK WORTHY OF THE LORD, PLEASE HIM, BEAR FRUIT AND GROW IN KNOWLEDGE OF GOD AFTER HE HAS GRANTED US THE "KNOWLEDGE OF HIS WILL IN ALL SPIRITUAL WISDOM AND UNDERSTANDING." THIS IS THE DIVINE ORDER OF THINGS.*

---

***Trying to "do the truth" will result in eventual failure, but heart belief will transform us -making it possible to do.***

If we try to "do the truth," we will eventually fail. However, when we believe the truth with our hearts, the truth will transform us into God's likeness. Heart belief that is truth, will produce the fruit of the Spirit without effort. It is only as the Spirit convinces us of the truth that we can believe it with our hearts. This is faith: being persuaded by the Spirit of the truth in my heart and believing it with absolute certainty.

To the degree that this is so, I will walk as Jesus walked. This takes us back to the correct order of things: believe first, walk second. Again, the Scriptures reveal this here: "...may [you] be filled with the knowledge of His will in all spiritual wisdom and understanding, SO THAT you will walk in a manner worthy of the Lord, to please Him in all respects, bearing fruit in every good work and increasing in the knowledge of God..." (Col. 1:9).

### *Intellectual Belief Will Only Take Us So Far in the process of Forgiving.*

Our intellectual belief regarding forgiving will only take us so far. Without the Spirit's persuasion of heart belief, we will not be able to forgive from the heart. Often, we try to force forgiveness based upon what we intellectually know that the Bible teaches. Forgiveness that is driven by our own will and determination alone will not produce true forgiveness. Nonetheless, this is probably the most common path we take.

The formula is basically this: 1) Deny what you feel (suppression), 2) Force a decision to forgive based on what you intellectually believe to be the truth, and 3) Keep denying (suppressing) what you feel, claiming the victory, and maintain the territory so that the enemy cannot convince you to "un-forgive"—as if that were a theological possibility.

Too often we hold to Biblical truths with our intellectual belief rather than with faith, or a heart belief. Forgiveness from the heart requires a "knowing" the truth that supersedes our intellectual understanding. Belief of the heart is truth that the Spirit bestows on us. When we know the truth with the heart (as it relates to forgiving those who have hurt us), we will, with the heart, forgive without effort.

It is the lies we harbor that are contrary to His perspective that keep us from forgiving. The hesitation and resistance we feel about forgiving is directly related to what we believe about forgiving. For example, if I believe that forgiving my offender allows him to get away with what he did, makes me vulnerable to be hurt again, or minimizes the offence, etc., then I am unlikely to forgive. These beliefs left unattended will keep me in bondage

### *Bearing the Fruit, NOT Doing the Fruit*

In the Colossians 1:9-10 passage, did you notice that one of the outcomes of God bestowing His truth upon us is "bearing fruit in every good work?" Too often, we try to "do the fruit" as opposed to bearing it. The Spirit's fruit consists of love, joy, peace, patience, kindness, goodness, gentleness, faithfulness, and self-control (Gal. 5:22-23). It is common to see believers attempting to mimic the fruit by trying to act it out; however, this is not a genuine expression of the life of Christ. The fruit of the Spirit is the fruit of the Spirit. It is not accomplished by man.

---

*Too often we spend much energy in trying to conform our behavior to the truth, as opposed to our being transformed by the it. These two are not the same; one self-accomplished while the latter is accomplished only by the Spirit.*

---

### *Fruit Not a TO-DO List*

The fruit of the Spirit is not a "TO-DO" list that we are called to try and accomplish. The fruit is the outcome of being "...filled with the knowledge of His will in all spiritual wisdom and understanding…" (Col. 1:9).

In TPM, we focus on transformation. Transformation is the expected outcome of God having persuaded us of His truth within our hearts. Transformation is made evident by the presence of the fruit of the Spirit. Trying to perform the fruit by our own effort is not transformation by the Spirit. Many believers spend much energy trying to conform their behavior to the truth, as opposed to allowing themselves to be transformed by the Truth. There is a big difference between the two.

It is possible to do what may resemble the fruit and yet not bear it. It would be unreasonable to suggest that an unbeliever could experience the fruit of the Spirit, since they do not know Christ. Yet there are many unbelievers who act in a loving, patient, kind, good, and gentle way, out of their own effort.

Only those who are connected to the Vine can bear the fruit (John 15:4-5) and it is only when we possess faith—truth in the heart by the persuasion of God—that we can "bear fruit in every good work." God alone bestows faith upon a person, He is the source of any truth we may hold in our hearts and He alone can produce good and lasting fruit.

When there is a change of the heart due to receiving knowledge of the truth, forgiveness flows effortlessly. When I am able to see things from God's perspective I can forgive as He has forgiven. God forgives because He always operates in the truth; He is the truth. Jesus forgave His abusers because He too operated in the truth. When we know the truth we too can forgive as Christ forgave since we are in Christ and have put on a new self that "... is being renewed to a true knowledge according to the image of the One who created him" (Col. 3:10).

### *Forgiveness in Africa*

I have been practicing the principles that are shared in this book for over two decades. I have witnessed the Lord grant His truth to untold numbers of people all around the globe. I have heard innumerable testimonies of unimaginable horror, pain, trauma and misery that had been acted out upon people. Forgiving such crimes would seem impossible, and yet I watched it occur spontaneously and without effort as each of these people came into the heart knowledge of the truth. Such forgiveness was not by their sheer willpower or ardent determination, but only because they were granted God's perspective and their heart beliefs were renewed with the truth.

Probably one of the most powerful testimonies I have heard concerning forgiveness came to me in an email some years ago (one of thousands of unsolicited testimonies our office receives). A young woman living in some part of Africa was fleeing with her family from a warring tribe who were slaughtering the people in her village. After running for their lives for many hours, they stopped at a vacant hut to try to get some needed rest. While they were sleeping, a group of men came upon them and forced them outside. One by one they took machetes and chopped each member of the family into pieces while making this young girl watch. They then proceeded to rape and torture her until morning. Thinking she was near death, they left her to die.

By God's grace she survived and eventually made her way to safety. She was taken in and cared for by a Christian couple who happened to be trained in TPM. After many months of recovery from her physical wounds and working through the natural process of grief, they began to minister to her using TPM. When they started, she was filled with anger and rage and only wanted revenge and justice. In session after session the Lord met her in her pain and poured a steady stream of truth and light into her broken heart and soul. Lie by lie and truth by truth, she came to embrace the Lord's perspective. As the truth transformed her, she slowly released the enormous "debt" these men incurred, because of the evil choices they made to hurt her.

This young lady sent me an email telling me her story, but what amazed me the most was the compassion she expressed for those who had murdered her family. I do not remember her exact words, but they were something like, "When I look at those memories, I only feel the love and peace of Christ. The anger and rage is all gone. When I think of those who killed my family, I feel a deep sadness for their souls. For those men to have done the evil they did, they must be very lost in their own pain and darkness. I pray for them and hope that they will find Jesus before it's too late." She could release the "debt" of her debtor with compassion, only because God had already released her.

***The time of the offense has no bearing on how we will forgive.***

Because forgiving has everything to do with heart belief, it really does not matter if the offense we experienced was in our childhood or last week at the workplace. The process and principles used to forgive are the same, as we will interpret life through the lens of our belief. We establish much of what we believe about ourselves and the world around us during childhood, especially before the age of twelve. These beliefs are our heart beliefs. Once these heart beliefs are taken into our hearts they remain ours throughout life, acting as the lens through which we interpret experiences we encounter in the future. However, God desires to fit us with new glasses of truth to correct our distorted perspective.

Once our lie-based beliefs are in place we will continually interpret each new life experience through these new lenses. If we are mistreated at the workplace, we will be more likely to interpret what happened to us through, [rather we will simply put on] our "glasses" we acquired many years before. We will likely misinterpret what may actually be happening in the present situation. So regardless of whether we are dealing with a childhood offense or a more recent experience, the process is the same. Therefore, the premise from which this book approaches forgiveness is this: difficulty in forgiving is relative to what we believe.

We have discovered that simply telling the person the truth rarely produces a successful outcome. If anything, it frustrates the person further to know the truth and yet be unable to comply with it. We believe that only God through His Spirit can change what we believe in our hearts. This is not something that we can do for ourselves by intellectual means. The challenge before us is to help the person identify the heart belief that is causing them to harbor resentment and find a means to replace the lies they believe with the truth. Unless the heart belief is replaced with the truth the struggle to forgive will remain.

This book takes a more general overview of the process of forgiving rather than dealing with a specific application of it. However, you will be exposed to the process we call Transformation Prayer Ministry (TPM) which is the approach we use when helping people to achieve genuine forgiveness. Training in this approach is freely available to you online. Through TPM we have seen many people successfully forgive from their heart and find the freedom that they desired. Whether you choose to apply TPM or not, we are convinced that forgiveness will be a continual struggle for those who harbor lie-based heart belief in relation to their forgiving. You are welcome to explore TPM as a possible approach you might take and choose to avail yourself of the training.

# *Discussion Questions*

1. How do you respond to the idea that genuine forgiveness is accomplished without effort as a natural outcome of our faith/purified heart belief?

2. Faith is described as something we possess as opposed to something that we do. It is because we possess faith that we are able to do what we do. For example, our trusting God is not faith, but rather an outcome of the faith we possess. Because we believe we trust. With this understanding of faith, how are good works, the fruit of the Spirit and forgiveness, fundamentally the same?

3. How does heart belief "surpass" knowledge? How can this reality impact us both positively and negatively?

4. How does Col. 1:9-10 speak to how you are seeking to live your Christian life?

   *"[be] ...filled with the knowledge of His will in all spiritual wisdom and understanding, <u>SO THAT</u> [we] will walk in a manner worthy of the Lord, to please Him in all respects, bearing fruit in every good work and increasing in the knowledge of God" (Col. 1:9-10)*

5. How do you understand and view the fruit of the Spirit? Is the fruit a "to do" list of tasks to accomplish, or that which ONLY God can bring about? How does your life and behavior reveal how you view the fruit?

6. How is it possible that an unbeliever can appear to express more good fruit than some believers? What is the difference between "doing" the fruit and "bearing" the fruit?

7. Many people spend much energy trying to conform their behavior to the truth as opposed to being transformed by the truth. Why do you think this is so? How is being transformed different from trying to mimic the life of Christ?

# Chapter Three

## Faith: The Persuasion of God

The Greek word used in the New Testament and translated as faith or belief is usually *pistis*. Depending on the context in which the word is used, it may be translated as trust, assurance, reliability, confidence, fidelity, or faithfulness. It is often used as a verb describing something being accomplished such as trusting someone, having confidence in someone or something, or being faithful.

However, the root word from which the word *pistis* is derived is *peitho*. Peitho has a different meaning than what is often implied with the word *pistis*. *Peitho* is primarily limited to two basic meanings of which are understood from the position or posture in which they are being applied. *Peitho* either means to *persuade or to be persuaded*. Faith is what happens when God persuades us of the truth within our hearts. Faith is also what we possess when we are persuaded of this truth within our hearts. It is peitho —the persuasion of God and our being persuaded— that we will focus our attention throughout this book.

---

*FAITH IS WHAT HAPPENS WHEN GOD PERSUADES US OF THE TRUTH WITHIN OUR HEARTS. FAITH IS ALSO WHAT WE POSSESS WHEN WE ARE PERSUADED OF THIS TRUTH WITHIN OUR HEARTS.*

---

Again, you might be wondering why we are discussing faith when the focus of this book is forgiveness. It is because heart belief is the essence of faith and without faith we cannot forgive from our hearts. As stated earlier, faith is something we possess as opposed to something that we do. It is because we possess faith that we do the works of faith; trust, depend upon, have confidence in, forgive, and etc.

When God persuades us of the truth in our hearts, we believe. This belief is our faith. It is because of this faith that we were made right with God (Rom. 10:10), and it is this same persuasion of the truth that is our continual victory since *"... this is the victory that has overcome the world-- our faith"* (1 Jo. 5:4). Only God can bring about this persuasion. Nobody, not even ourselves, can persuade us of the truth within our hearts. We can be persuaded intellectually by others, but no one can persuade us of the truth in our hearts other than the Spirit.

### We Either Forgive or Don't Forgive Because of Heart Belief.

God is only interested in actions that are based on faith. Works that are the outcome of our own effort and determination are not from faith. This goes back to the "SO THAT" found at the beginning of Colossians 1:10. It is ONLY because God has filled [us] with *"... the knowledge of His will in all spiritual wisdom and understanding..."* SO THAT we can *"... walk in a manner worthy of the Lord, to please Him in all respects, bearing fruit in every good work and increasing in the knowledge of God; strengthened with all power, according to His glorious might, for the attaining of all steadfastness and patience; joyously giving thanks to the Father, who has qualified us to share in the inheritance of the saints in Light"* (Col. 1:9-12).

There is no exception to this. There is no workaround. If we are not walking in faith—knowing the truth in our hearts as an absolute certainty—our works are dead works and not the fruit which results from faith in God (Heb. 6:1).

Faith and forgiveness go hand in hand just as the act of forgiving falls into the category of "good works" in which God predestined us to walk. These good works are not achieved through our own effort and determination or ardent obedience, but rather as an outflow of Christ in us, the fruit of His Spirit. This is why trying to forgive by willful choosing, denying our feelings and obeying the truth has such a poor success rate. It is not from faith. In the same way we cannot "do the fruit" and try to be more patient, kind, good, etc., we cannot forgive from the heart apart from knowing the truth within our heart.

### *Bearing Good Works Rather than Doing Them*

The "good works" in which God is interested are only those He has brought about Himself and not those of our own doing. This work is very similar to the great salvation He bestowed upon us through His grace and faith. We know that salvation is not of works, but only of grace and through faith. Most believers would agree on this point: salvation is the outcome of God's work alone and *"...not of ourselves so that no one may boast..."* And although the Scriptures are clear that living the Christian life is accomplished by the same faith that established it, it is not uncommon to see believers attempting to live it out by works. The Scriptures say clearly, *"... as you have received Christ Jesus the Lord, so walk in Him"* (Col. 2:6).

In the same way that we entered into this new covenant relationship through Christ and *"...have obtained our introduction by faith into this grace in which we stand..."* (Rom. 5:2), He too *"... will perfect it until the day of Christ Jesus"* (Phil. 1:6). God began the work, He is doing the work, and He will finish it. We are not doing works, but rather bearing fruit. As Jesus said, *"I am the vine, you are the branches; he who abides in Me and I in him, he bears much* *fruit, for apart from Me you can do <u>nothing</u>"* (Jn. 15:5).

### *"Without faith it is impossible to please Him..." (Heb. 11:6)*

The Bible says *"...without faith it is impossible to please Him, for he who comes to God must believe that He is and that He is a rewarder of those who seek Him"* (Heb. 11:6). Depending on which Bible commentary you read, the interpretation of this passage will vary. Since faith is the determining factor of whether we please God or not, in this study we will approach this passage from the root meaning of faith: *peitho - to persuade or be persuaded.*

First, the word *IMPOSSIBLE* screams out at us. The passage tells us that faith is the only way to please God. Nothing we do, no matter how hard we try or how high we jump, pleases God—unless it is by faith. This, by itself, is enough to take the wind out of our sails if we are trying to perform for God.

It's a real temptation for us to focus on pleasing God through our efforts and to try to be like Jesus. We think, "What would Jesus do?" We tend to have a "stop doing this and start doing that" approach to pleasing God. The first issue with this approach is that controlled behavior is not of faith, and the second issue follows: because it is not of faith, it does not please God.

Someone may wish to remind me that *"Faith without works is dead"* (Ja. 2:26), but again, there are different interpretations of this scripture, depending on which commentary you read. However, using *peitho* as our filter for interpretation, let's allow the passage to speak for itself.

### *Peitho-Faith Produces Good Works, the Fruit of the Spirit.*

We have already seen that when we have faith (heart belief), the fruit will follow. I believe this is what James was arguing in this passage. He was not telling us to go out and do good works to prove we have faith, but to demonstrate that *peitho*-faith will bear fruit or produce good works, and this fruit affirms we do have faith. When I am persuaded (*peitho*) of the truth by God's Spirit, the works that follow will be "good works" instead of "dead works." It is also because I know the truth that I can forgive.

### *Without Faith, "Trust and Obey" is Nothing but Wearisome.*

When I was a child we used to sing the old hymn "Trust and Obey." The words declared, "Trust and obey for there's no other way to be happy in Jesus, but to trust and obey." As much as I still love that old song, there is yet something more needed. Blind obedience alone will only carry us so far. It also makes for a worn-out and weary follower of Christ. Too often we expend great effort in trying to do the truth, while not believing it. Because most believers hold much knowledge of the Scriptures, they know what is expected of them. However, doing the truth that they know is often a struggle. However, when we know the truth with the heart, trust, works, forgiveness, etc. are all a natural and expected outcome and requires no effort to do or maintain. Knowing the truth with the heart produces good works which are an expression of the fruit of the Spirit.

---

*Blind obedience alone will only carry us so far. It also makes for a worn-out and weary follower of Christ. However, when we know the truth with the heart, trust is a natural and expected outcome and requires no effort to do or maintain.*

---

The missing component here is faith. Throughout this book I have defined faith as "believing the truth with the heart with absolute certainty." We can only have this faith because God has persuaded us of it. When He persuades us of the truth within our hearts, we believe. Heart belief in the truth removes all doubt. It goes beyond hope to the *"assurance of things hoped for"* and it is not blind obedience, but rather the *"conviction of things NOT seen"* (Heb. 11:1). Trust is what we do because we possess faith. Faith —truth believed with the heart—is given by God and culminates in our trust of Him.

People typically limit their understanding of faith as something they choose to exercise, such as, "putting their faith in God" or as the song states, "Just trust and obey." The problem here is that trying hard to "trust and obey" without faith is laborious, wearisome, and lifeless. Faith is knowing the truth that God has persuaded us of with absolute certainty. Genuine faith contains no measure of doubting. Doubt is the evidence of believing something contrary to the truth. It is only when I possess faith (heart belief) that I can do things such as trust and obey. Genuinely trusting God is only possible because we already possess faith. Trust follows as an outcome of this faith. It is only because God has put His faith (persuasion of the truth) into us, that we are able to trust Him. If I did not already believe in my heart that God is trustworthy, then I could not really trust Him.

---

*GENUINELY TRUSTING GOD IS ONLY POSSIBLE IF WE ALREADY POSSESS FAITH. TRUST FOLLOWS AS AN OUTCOME OF THIS FAITH. IT IS ONLY BECAUSE GOD HAS PUT HIS FAITH (PERSUASION OF THE TRUTH) INTO US, THAT WE ARE ABLE TO TRUST HIM. FAITH IS NOT WHAT WE DO, BUT WHAT WE POSSESS. IT IS BECAUSE WE POSSESS THE GIFT OF FAITH (BEING PERSUADED OF THE TRUTH) THAT WE ARE ABLE TO TRUST AND OBEY.*

---

Trusting God is an outflow or fruit of our faith, but it is not faith itself. Our faith is what we believe in our hearts as an outcome of being persuaded of it by God. If we limit our definition of faith to something that we can achieve in our own strength, then the idea of God granting us faith may seem strange.

Faith is not what we do, but what we possess. It is because we possess the gift of faith (being persuaded of the truth) that we are able to trust and obey.

### *Grace and faith are gifts from God*

One of the clearest explanations of how a person comes into the saving knowledge of Christ is expressed in the passage that says, *"For by grace you have been saved through faith; and that not of yourselves, it is the gift of God; not as a result of works, so that no one may boast. For we are His workmanship, created in Christ Jesus for good works, which God prepared beforehand so that we would walk in them"* (Eph. 2:8-10)

If we approach this passage with the understanding that faith is something that *we do*, as opposed to a gift that which *God has granted*, a glaring contradiction becomes apparent. This understanding would render the passage to say, *"For by grace are you saved <u>because you chose to trust</u> in Christ..."* which stands in conflict with what follows, *"Not of yourselves...not of works..."* Choosing to trust would be a "work" accomplished by something that I was doing.

However, if faith is bestowed upon us just as grace, and not something we do, but something we possess, then it makes perfect sense to hear that grace and faith are both a *"...gift of God..."* and that *"...no one can boast.."* concerning the grace or the faith we have been given. Salvation is a gift of God and not conditional upon anything that we might do. According to the Scriptures we are saved because we believe, not because of what we do, *"...with the heart a person believes, resulting in righteousness..."* (Rom. 10:10). It is because we are the blessed recipients of His grace and faith that we are then able to trust Him and do the good works *"...which God prepared beforehand so that we would walk in them."* We are indeed *"...His workmanship, created in Christ Jesus for good works..."*

We cannot trust Him unless we believe that He is trustworthy. We cannot believe unless He persuades us of the truth. We cannot do genuine good works unless He produces them in us since the good works are a fruit of His Spirit. When we believe with the heart trust and fruit will follow.

---

*We cannot trust Him unless we believe that He is trustworthy. We cannot believe unless He persuades us of the truth. We cannot do genuine good works unless He produces them in us since the good works are a fruit of His Spirit. When we believe with the heart trust and fruit will follow.*

---

Remember the meaning of *peitho*; to either persuade or to be persuaded. God persuades us and we are persuaded. We are still required to put our trust in the truth of the Gospel, but it is only because we first believe it that we can then trust in it. It is because we believe that we trust. It is impossible to put our trust in someone or something that we do not believe. If I do not believe what you are telling me, I cannot trust you. Unless I first believe you, I cannot trust you. Trust is the outcome of my belief.

### *Who is doing what, when it comes to works?*

The passage goes on to say that we were predestined for "good works," but these "good works" are no more accomplished by us than was our salvation. These are also the outcome of God's grace and faith (See Galatians 3:1-3).

---

*The "good works" in which God is interested are only those He has brought about Himself and not those of our own doing.*

---

Our salvation was not obtained through our works and neither are the "good works" that follow living the Christian life. They are not accomplished through our own doing, but are an outcome of God's grace and faith. Jesus said plainly, *"Apart from Me you can do nothing"* (Jo. 15:5). The truth is, we can do things that look like the fruit of the Spirit, but we cannot bear fruit apart from the vine. There is a major difference between bearing fruit and trying to do fruit, even though the outcome may look similar in appearance. Those around us may not be able to distinguish between the two, but God can clearly see the difference.

Forgiveness is the outcome of grace and faith as is our salvation. In the same way that God persuaded my heart of the Gospel and I believed (Rom. 10:10), so too the Spirit persuades me of the truth about forgiveness and I forgive.

It is the purified heart belief, which God has brought about, that makes it possible for us to consider forgiving. When the Spirit releases us from our lie-based heart belief we will no longer need the "solutions" we have established to protect ourselves, which hinder us from releasing those against whom we are embittered. It is God desire to free us of both our lie-based heart belief as well as our *solution* beliefs.

If I believe a lie in my heart about forgiving, then I will not forgive. My heart belief is my faith, but not all faith is pure. This is why our faith needs to be refined and made pure (Ja. 1:3, 1 Pet 4:12-13, 1 Pet. 1:7). The refinement of our faith and renewal of our minds is the pathway to walking in the Spirit and expressing His fruit. Forgiveness is brought about in the same way.

In Transformation Prayer Ministry we refer to this as transformation; the expected outcome of a purified faith. When God grants us His truth, renewing our minds, we will bear or produce good works in the same manner that we bear the fruit of the Spirit. The fruit and good works are proven evidence that transformation has occurred within our hearts.

When God persuades us of His truth through His Spirit, a purified faith will be the outcome. In other words, we are persuaded by Him and, therefore, believe the truth. With this understanding, we see that the ability to believe is not dependent on our own endeavor, but rather on God's persuasion of the truth within our hearts. A pure faith originates with God, since He is the one doing the persuading. It culminates in those who have been persuaded or convinced of the truth.

### *What might Calvin and Arminius say?*

Who could possibly refuse this wonderful gift of grace and faith if God has persuaded them of the truth? This depends on your theological position. People typically fall into one of two camps (or a mix of both), in what is known as either Calvinism or Arminianism. (You can do a more in-depth study on these two views later.) In brief, Calvinism holds the position that God's grace is irresistible. A pure Calvinist would say that if God chooses to persuade you of the truth then you would not be able to resist it and it would melt any hardened heart. Arminianism would say that it is possible to resist the grace of God and choose to reject the gift even though the truth of it is believed. A Calvinist would argue that when God calls a person to salvation and persuades him of its validity, that person will have no other option but come to salvation. This would be considered "irresistible grace." A true Arminian would reject this premise.

This is the subject of a different discussion and worth looking into, if you do not already hold a position on the matter. You may already do so, but may not know with which of these two camps you are most aligned. The truth is, there is much diversity in the body of Christ. You will find many versions of both Calvinism and Arminianism, but the truth probably lies somewhere between the two.

Although I believe that the Bible in its original form was without error, I do not think that a perfect interpretation (or theology) of the Bible exists. All systems of theology fall short of explaining that which cannot be totally understood. We are simply incapable of fully grasping the truth as it is understood by God. We cannot know the mind or the ways of God since His thoughts and ways are as far as the heaven is from the earth compared to ours (Isa. 55:8-13). But then, that is why He is God and we are human. However, this gives cause for us to hold loosely some of these debatable issues and strive toward unity that centers on Christ.

What we would like you to consider here is the *way* in which we come to believe anything. Believing is not something that we wake up one day and decide to do, but rather it is because of *peitho/persuasion*. We have been persuaded to believe what we believe. We only believe something (theological or secular) because someone (or some information source) has persuaded us of its validity. We only believe what we do because we have been persuaded that it is the truth.

---

*BELIEVING IS NOT SOMETHING THAT WE WAKE UP ONE DAY AND DECIDE TO DO, BUT RATHER IT IS BECAUSE OF PEITHO/PERSUASION. WE HAVE BEEN PERSUADED TO BELIEVE WHAT WE BELIEVE. WE ONLY BELIEVE SOMETHING (THEOLOGICAL OR SECULAR) BECAUSE SOMEONE (OR SOME INFORMATION SOURCE) HAS PERSUADED US OF ITS VALIDITY. WE ONLY BELIEVE WHAT WE DO BECAUSE WE HAVE BEEN PERSUADED THAT IT IS THE TRUTH.*

---

This being the case, we believe that it is the Spirit who convinces us through His persuasion of the truth to believe the Gospel. It is only because He has persuaded us of the truth of the Gospel that we choose to trust in it. Whether we can *"...exchange this truth for a lie..."* (Rom. 1:25) once we believe it, is a theological position that you can work through at a later time. Calvin would say not possible, whereas Arminius would say absolutely!

The Apostle Paul reveals that the unbeliever is where he is because of his ignorance of the truth and the hardness of his heart. He said, *"...walk no longer just as the Gentiles also walk, in the futility of their mind, being darkened in their understanding, excluded from the life of God because of the ignorance that is in them, because of the hardness of their heart..."* (Eph. 4:17-18). Here we must ask, how did the unbeliever get to this place? Why is he ignorant of the truth and how was his heart hardened? Again, this is something that you will need to study on your own as it is not the focus of this book..

According to the Scriptures, all people have been given some measure of the truth (Rom. 1:18-19). The question is, what have they done with what they have been given. Each of us will someday give an account for all that God has given us and how we used it. In the first chapter of the book of Romans we see a progressive slide down the slippery slope of depravity. However, the slope begins with the person knowing the truth and "suppressing the truth in unrighteousness..." and progressively "exchanging the truth for a lie..."

It is possible that a person could be given the truth and yet not believe that it was true. He could take the truth that he was given and choose to believe a lie instead. In practice, this action would constitute "exchanging the truth for a lie." However, it seems illogical for someone to put any effort into suppressing or rejecting a belief unless they thought it was the truth. If they thought it was a lie, then they would have no need to suppress or deny it. These people described in the following passage are exchanging the truth that has been given them for that which is not true and it appears that they initially knew it was the truth.

Take the time to read Romans 1: 18-32 and notice how unrighteous men were given truth by God, but suppressed it, rejected it and exchanged it for a lie. However, notice also that they did not "choose to believe" the truth they were given, but rather suppressed and rejected it, despite knowing it.

All these issues raise questions worth our attention in another discussion at another time. Nonetheless, the point I am trying to make is this; faith is something that we possess because God has bestowed it upon us. We possess faith, we do not produce it. Walking in faith flows from possessing faith. Because we possess faith we can walk in faith, without effort. If it is a struggle for us to "walk in faith" then we are not really operating in faith. The struggle is rooted in our unbelief. Faith is believing the truth with absolute certainty. However, belief is not something that we can just choose to do, again, it requires that we be persuaded of it. When we know the truth within our hearts in this manner, good works and the Spirit's fruit are the natural and expected outcome of this faith. If we are having to try to do these things, then we do not yet believe it in our hearts.

### *Faith and Works*

James the Apostle said it this way, *"...I will show you my faith by my works"* (Ja. 2:18). It was because of the faith he possessed that his works followed. His works were evidence of the faith he possessed. Consider this in relation to the fruit of the Spirit.

Because God has persuaded me of the following truth and I believe it with absolute certainty, the fruit is present in my life. The fruit is manifested through the "good works" that we were destined to accomplish because of what God has done. *"For we are God's handiwork, created in Christ Jesus to do good works, which God prepared in advance for us to do"* (Eph. 2:10).

It is because God has granted us His truth that we are able to do "good works". The Apostle Paul prayed that we would be *"…filled with the knowledge of His will in all spiritual wisdom and understanding, SO THAT [we would] walk in a manner worthy of the Lord, to please Him in all respects, bearing fruit in every good work and increasing in the knowledge of God…"* (Col. 1:9-10). *"He granted"* so that *"we might do."*

Now to return to the declaration made by James the Apostle, *"faith without works is dead."* This is preceded by the following illustration, *"… if a brother or sister is without clothing and in need of daily food, and one of you says to them, 'Go in peace, be warmed and be filled,' and yet you do not give them what is necessary for their body, what use is that? Even so faith, if it has no works, is dead, being by itself"* (Ja. 2:15-17).

Here we see a problem: even though the person says "Go in peace, be warmed and be filled," since there is no action accompanying the person's words, it comes across as nonsense; there is no value in what he has said.

This is where it's easy to confuse intellectual knowledge of the truth with *peitho*-faith. We can believe it is God's will that we care for the needy and attend to the basic necessities of our brothers and sisters in Christ, but if we do nothing when we see them in need, we do not have heart-belief, only mental assent to the truth.

This is also where it gets tricky. If I happen to feel badly about not doing the right thing and I just choose to do it because the Bible "tells me so," this action is not faith but dead works flowing from a dead faith. God is not pleased with dead works. He desires that we operate naturally and effortlessly from the truth He has given us within our hearts, which is an expression of Christ's Spirit within us: the fruit of the Spirit. This is why performance-based spirituality is not faith and does not please God. God is looking for those whose hearts are persuaded of the truth. The old prophet declared, *"The Lord's eyes keep on roaming throughout the earth, looking for those whose hearts completely belong to him, so that he may strongly support them"* (2 Chr. 16:9).

If we believe that caring for our brothers and sisters is God's will, and we believe this truth in our hearts, we will have no other thought than to clothe and feed them. The truth will produce the fruit of the Spirit of kindness, goodness, gentleness, etc. and we will act accordingly. It is easy to confuse bearing good fruit that comes from being persuaded of the truth with obedience that flows from an intellectual knowledge of the truth. Even unbelievers can obey the truth if they choose to, but they cannot bear its fruit.

Does this mean that God is only pleased with me if my faith is perfected and entirely pure? Not at all. First, there is a difference between God being pleased *with us* and Him being pleased *with what we do*. We know that God is ultimately pleased with us because of the atoning work of Christ. Since God is pleased with Jesus, if we are in Christ, then God is also pleased with us. When our good works are motivated by a purified faith, He finds additional pleasure in what we do.

Without question, we will never attain a perfected faith while on this earth but only a faith that is being purified measure-by-measure. It is the works that flow from the truth believed by the heart with which God is pleased. Works motivated by lie-based belief—though they look very similar to those motivated by truth-based belief—are not pleasing to God. Even though we may not be able to distinguish one from the other, God has no difficulty doing so since He sees the motive of the heart (Pro. 16:2).

When it comes to "good works" God is pleased with *why* we do what we do as opposed to what we do; that is, He is pleased when our works are motivated by purified heart belief; genuine faith. The Scriptures state it this way, *"...the only thing that counts is faith expressing itself through love"* (Gal. 5:6). If we use the definition for faith that I have suggested, a paraphrase of this passage might be stated as, *"...the only thing that counts is the truth believed with absolute certainty with the heart, which has found its expression through love."*

---

*WHEN IT COMES TO "GOOD WORKS" GOD IS PLEASED WITH <u>WHY</u> WE DO WHAT WE DO MORE SO THAN WHAT WE DO; THAT IS, HE IS PLEASED WHEN OUR WORKS ARE MOTIVATED BY PURIFIED HEART BELIEF; GENUINE FAITH. "...THE ONLY THING THAT COUNTS IS FAITH EXPRESSING ITSELF THROUGH LOVE" (GAL. 5:6).*

---

### Salvation and Faith

Because trust is the outcome of belief, I am concerned that some people who have assumed they are Christians may, in fact, not be Christians at all. If our belief is that we are saved because of something we have done or something we are doing, and it is not because the Spirit has persuaded us of the truth resulting in our trust and obedience, then we may be in trouble. Heart belief is how we enter the family of God, for it is *"...with the heart a person believes, resulting in righteousness..."* (Rom. 10:10). Trusting in Christ (what we do) is only possible because we have been persuaded of the truth and believed.

---

*IF OUR BELIEF IS THAT WE ARE SAVED BECAUSE OF SOMETHING WE HAVE DONE OR SOMETHING WE ARE DOING, AND IT IS NOT BECAUSE THE SPIRIT HAS PERSUADED US OF THE TRUTH RESULTING IN OUR TRUST AND OBEDIENCE, THEN WE MAY BE IN TROUBLE.*

---

Well-meaning evangelists have often led people to believe that they are saved by simply praying the "sinner's prayer" and "choosing" to trust in Jesus.

Salvation is the outcome of belief with the heart *"...for with the heart a person believes, resulting in righteousness"* (Rom. 10:10). We cannot trust unless we first believe. We cannot believe unless God shines His light into our hearts persuading us of the truth. Trusting Christ is the outcome of believing the truth of the Gospel. Belief comes first, followed by trusting. Salvation is initiated by God and completed by God. No part of it is *"...a result of works, so that no one may boast"* (Eph. 2:9).

When God persuaded us of the truth of the Gospel, we believed. *"For God...made His light shine in our hearts to give us the light of the knowledge of God's glory displayed in the face of Christ"* (2 Cor. 4:6). It is because God has shone His light into our hearts that we believe. It is God's persuasion of the truth in our hearts that results in our salvation. Just having a person pray the "sinner's prayer" and asking them to somehow try to believe, provides no guarantee saving faith will occur.

Again, it is because we have believed that we trust. We believe because we have been persuaded of the truth by the Spirit. No one believes something by deciding to believe it. We receive the information in question from some person or source, and if we are convinced that it is true, we believe it. We do not believe because we decide to, but only because we are persuaded *(peitho)* that what is being offered is true. We enter God's salvation because He convinces us of the truth and we are persuaded of it. It is because we believe that we can trust and obey.

### *Forgiving from the Heart*

You may have already seen how this discussion applies to our study on forgiveness in various ways. Forgiveness is a work that is accomplished from the heart. If we approach it from an intellectual perspective—what the Bible says—we will encounter much struggle. Choosing to forgive just because it is the right and obedient thing to do rarely works.

Forgiveness is certainly called for and expected from us, but just as the fruit of the Spirit is a byproduct of faith—believing the truth with the heart with absolute certainty—so too, forgiving is an *effortless* byproduct, or expected outcome, of knowing the truth with the heart. When our heart belief is contrary to forgiving, then forgiveness is not likely to come about. However, when the Spirit persuades us of the truth about those who have offended us and releases us from the lies hindering us from releasing the debt, forgiveness will occur *effortlessly*. When our heart is persuaded of the truth, we can forgive from the heart. When we know the truth with our heart we can forgive with the heart. If our heart belief is contrary to forgiving, then we will not be able to release others from their debt.

## *Discussion Questions*

1. How *is peitho-fa*ith (persuading or being persuaded) different from the way you may have understood faith before? How does faith differ from trust? Which comes first?

2. What is the difference between being persuaded of the truth with the heart and believing the truth intellectually?

3. Why is faith (heart belief) crucial for forgiving the debts of those who have offended us? How can lie-based heart belief hinder us from forgiving?

4. Why is the "SO THAT" found in Colossians 1:9-10 important for our understanding faith and good works?

5. What might hinder us from being a "bearer" of good works? Is there a difference between being a "bearer" of good works and being a "doer" of good works? If so, how would you explain it.

6. According to Colossians *1:9-10, we are to "... walk in a manner worthy of the Lord to please Him in all respects…"* However, this is only after *we have been "... filled with the knowledge of His will in all spiritual wisdom* and understanding…" Is it possible to "walk" and "serve the Lord" without having this knowledge?

7. What might trying to "walk" without our "being filled with the knowledge" look like and what are the ramifications of attempting to live the Christian life in this fashion?

8. Does it feel true to you, or even possible that *forgiveness* will occur effortlessly after the Spirit has persuaded us of the truth about those who have offended us and released us from the lies we harbor, which are hindering us from the debt? What are the reasons for your answer?

9. Why is ardent obedience insufficient for living a life of faith? Hint: Faith is believing the truth with the heart with absolute certainty producing good works. What part does persuasion play in our coming to believe something?

# Chapter Four

## Principles of Forgiveness in Matthew 18

The previous few chapters were intended to lay down a foundation upon which we will now build. We will continue the remaining discussion by looking at what we call the "Principles of Forgiveness." These principles are drawn from Matthew, chapter 18, where Jesus tells the story of the indebted servant and the compassionate King. Jesus' primary intention was to declare how great a forgiveness God has for those who will receive it. Within this passage there are also principles that we can glean and apply as we seek to forgive.

### *The Forgiveness Quota: How Many Times Must I Forgive Someone?*

Though there are principles of forgiveness found throughout the Scriptures, in the remainder of this book we will focus our attention primarily on this specific passage. We will also continue to draw from the principles of Transformation Prayer Ministry as we consider how to forgive.

In Matthew 18:21-22, Jesus taught the disciples about genuine forgiveness when Peter asked, "*...how often shall my brother sin against me and I forgive him?*" Quite unexpectedly Jesus responded, "*I tell you, not seven times, but seven times seventy...*" I can almost see Peter's shoulders slump at this point. Peter may have asked Jesus this question because he had someone in mind whom he had already tried to forgive many times, or he may have been looking for Jesus to provide him with a "forgiveness quota" that would release him from his obligation to continue to forgive. We may not know Peter's true motive in asking his question, but we do know that Jesus uses this opportunity to teach His disciples about this difficult subject.

Jesus responded with this story:

> *"For this reason, the kingdom of heaven may be compared to a certain king who wished to settle accounts with his slaves. And when he had begun to settle them, there was brought to him one who owed him ten thousand talents. But since he did not have the means to repay, his lord commanded him to be sold, along with his wife and children and all that he had, and repayment to be made. The slave therefore, falling down, prostrated himself before him, saying, 'Have patience with me, and I will repay you everything.' And the lord of that slave felt compassion and released him and forgave him the debt. But that slave went out and found one of his fellow slaves who owed him a hundred denarii; and he seized him and began to choke him, saying, 'Pay back what you owe.' So, his fellow slave fell down and began to entreat him, saying, 'Have patience with me and I will repay you.' He was unwilling however, but went and threw him in prison until he should pay back what was owed"* (Matt. 18:23-30).

This passage is traditionally interpreted as a demonstration of the great love and compassion God has for us and the forgiveness He offers to all who come to Him. In the first verse of the passage, Jesus is contrasting the heavenly perspective (the Kingdom of Heaven) with Peter's earthly perspective. He is basically saying, "Let me compare your understanding of forgiveness with the way it is understood in the Kingdom of Heaven." *We fully concur that this is the literal meaning and the intended purpose of this narrative.* But this passage also provides some important insight into why and how we should forgive the debts of those who have offended us.

First, to repeat a word of caution—genuine forgiveness rarely occurs by simply "choosing" to forgive. That path is seldom successful. As I have said, people will try hard to "do the right thing" and forgive, but the results rarely last. Yet, thankfully, this portion of Matthew 18 reveals a series of principles that can enable us to genuinely forgive the debts of those who have hurt us.

### *Aphiemy: A Cutting Off, Not a Restoration*

The Greek verb in the New Testament for "forgive" is *aphiemy*. The root meaning of this word is "to cut off, sever, release or send away." Too often we confuse forgiveness with reconciliation, or the restoration of a relationship. These are not one and the same. In Matthew 18, the king forgave the servant's debt, but the passage does not imply that reconciliation of the relationship occurred. Forgiveness is no guarantee that there will be any change in the relationship after it is given. Although forgiveness could positively impact the one forgiven, it may just as easily inflame him and result in more offensive behavior. We will soon discover that when forgiveness releases a person's debt, it also brings freedom, and thus releases the one who offers the forgiveness.

---

*WHEN FORGIVENESS RELEASES A PERSON'S DEBT, IT ALSO BRINGS FREEDOM, AND THUS RELEASES THE ONE WHO OFFERS THE FORGIVENESS.*

---

### *Why the Money Analogy?*

I believe that Jesus used the financial analogy to explain forgiveness, rather than using something more relational, in order to underscore the distinction between forgiveness and reconciliation. The relationship I have with my bank is not personal. I am not friends with the bank president or even the loan officer. Either may give me a cup of coffee now and then when I do business with them, but that is about as far as it goes. We meet merely around the issue of money. The cards or letters I receive from them are not personal or relational, but simply reminders about my loan or an invitation to borrow more money. Thus, ours would not be described as a personal relationship.

### *The One Forgiving Holds All the Power in the Matter*

If I were to default on my loan, the only "reconciliation" would be the bank's attempt to get their money back. They would not be working on restoring a friendship, but only on minimizing a financial loss. If I could not repay the amount due, they might decide to write off my loan and forgive the debt. But if they did so, it would not be on a personal or relational basis. The bank would only be forgiving the debt and not me personally. Forgiving my debt would not reconcile a relationship; it would only free me of my financial obligation.

I would probably have no part in the decision to forgive the debt. My input would not be necessary. I could file a complaint, but that would have no effect on their decision. If they did decide to forgive the debt, it would be forgiven. The moment they wiped it off the books, whether I had requested this or not, I would be debt free—the debt would be forgiven.

In Matthew 18 the king "forgave him the debt." Thus, it was the debt that was forgiven and not the slave himself. Nothing changed relationally between the slave and the king when the debt was cancelled. However, the ownership of the debt was transferred. By forgiving the debt, the King took it upon himself. Although the debt was forgiven, the debt (the loss of money) remained; the king assumed the weight of the unpaid debt. The money was still lost and would never return. This is true whenever someone forgives anyone for anything. Even though we forgive the debt of wrongful things done to us, forgiveness does not remove the wrong committed, it just releases the one who committed the offense from any obligation.

This is the forgiveness we see at the cross of Jesus. He took upon Himself the sins (the debt) of the world. By doing so, the "certificate of debt" was nailed to the cross: "*...having canceled out the certificate of debt consisting of decrees against us, which was hostile to us; and He has taken it out of the way, having nailed it to the cross*" (Col. 2:14). Forgiveness is the act of taking something away, not restoring a relationship. Remember, the Greek word for forgiveness is *apheimy*—to sever or cut off. God's forgiveness is not an act of restoring something broken, His forgiveness of sin is the act of cutting it off, and taking it away. Jesus' death resolved our debt to God so that we might be reconciled to Him as well. However, the forgiveness did not bring about the reconciliation, but only made it possible.

The next chapters will identify and explain the basic principles of forgiveness that are found in Matthew 18. Jesus encouraged Peter to forgive those who wronged him "seven times seventy," that is, over and over again. The same is asked of us. Why is it so difficult to do? We will discover the answer to this soon.

## *Pause and Review*

Before we look at the basic principles of forgiveness based upon Matthew 18 in the following chapter, a review of some of the basic concepts we have learned thus far might be helpful. Read through the following bullet points and try to recall the concepts you would have learned in the previous chapters. If you deemed what you read in the earlier chapters to be valuable, yet have not retained all that you had hoped to, please consider reading the information again. Only what you retain will travel with you in the days ahead.

- Forgiveness is not the outcome of strong determination, willpower or simply choosing to do it. Trying harder to forgive will not bring about the result we are looking for.

- Difficulty in forgiving is totally related to what we believe. Until we are able to view our situation from God's heavenly perspective it will be a struggle for us. Any perspective that is not God's is a false one even when our own feels like the truth.

- It is not what has happened to us that produces our emotional pain. Our belief is always the reason why we feel what we feel and then generally do what we do.

- If we try to overcome our bad feelings, suppress them, deny them or attempt to distract ourselves from them, this will hinder the very purpose for which God designed them.

- Negative emotion is a friend pointing out to us what we believe in our hearts. If we deny or reject what we feel we are ignoring the very means that God has designed to point out our falsehood.

- We always feel whatever we believe. There is no "work-a-round" for this consistent principle.

- No person or life situation is causing us to feel anything that we are feeling. Blaming others or our situation for what we feel keeps us in a perpetual loop of bondage.

- It is possible to believe the truth intellectually while believing a lie with our hearts. (Remember double-mindedness.) We can know what the Bible says concerning forgiveness and yet not be able to do it.

- Forgiving from the heart necessitates believing the truth with the heart. It is our contrary lie-based heart belief that keeps us from forgiving.

- Heart belief always overrides intellectual belief. This is why we can know the Bible verse that "God will supply all of our needs…" (Phil 4:19) and yet worry over our finances. We are admonished by the Scriptures to "…know the <u>love of Christ which</u> surpasses knowledge, that you may be filled up to all the fullness of God" (Eph. 3:19).

- Forgiveness is a work of God resulting from the transformation brought about by His renewal of our heart belief by the truth. (Rom. 12:2)

- Our heart beliefs are the "glasses" we wear through which we interpret life's situations and circumstances. As long as our "glasses" are lie-based we will continue to look through distorted lenses.

- Faith is the outcome of being persuaded by God of the truth within our hearts. This persuasion (peitho) is the faith God has granted and that we can possess as He bestows it upon us. (Eph. 1:17-18)

- Heart belief is the essence of faith. Faith is believing something with the heart with an absolute certainty. However, not all that we believe is the truth. Nevertheless, whatever we believe in our heart is our faith. This is why we need our faith purified. (1 Pet. 4:12-13)

- Forgiveness is like the fruit of the Spirit in that only God can bring it about. We can bear fruit, but we cannot produce it. (Col. 1:9-10)

- We were destined to walk in "good works" as an outcome of God's workmanship. Works are the outcome of our faith, that is, being persuaded by the Spirit within our hearts of His truth. It is from this persuasion of God that we can *do the good works that we do. "For we are His workmanship, created in Christ Jesus for good works, which God prepared beforehand* so that we would walk in them." (Eph. 2:10)

Forgiveness, like the fruit of the Spirit, is a good work that God has "prepared beforehand" that we should walk in. We are only able to bear His fruit because of the work that He has done. It is because of what He has done that we "… bear fruit in every good work…" (Col. 1:9-10)

- Our lie-based heart belief is the source of much of the negative pain in our lives including; worry, shame, fear, powerlessness, helplessness and abandonment, etc. However, we also believe other lies that are the basis of the solutions for the perceived problems we are trying to solve, and which are created by our lie-based heart beliefs. These solution beliefs are often accompanied by emotions that are members of the anger family: hate, revenge, bitterness, resentment, rancor, hostility, etc.

- Until both the heart belief and solution beliefs are renewed with the truth by the Spirit, forgiveness will remain elusive.

- There is a divine order that cannot be overlooked when it comes to forgiveness. Unless God grants us His truth, we cannot know it with the heart. Unless we know the truth, we cannot walk in it or bear His fruit. God does what He *does so that we may do what we do.*

> *"be filled with the knowledge of His will in all spiritual wisdom and understanding, **so that** you will walk in a manner worthy of the Lord, to please Him in all respects, bearing fruit in every good work and increasing in the knowledge of God; strengthened with all power, according to His glorious might, for the attaining of all steadfastness and patience; joyously giving thanks to the Father, who has qualified us to share in the inheritance of the saints in Light" (Col. 1:9-12)*

## *Discussion Questions*

1. Does understanding that t*he Greek* word translated as "forgive" is aphiemy, meaning to sever or cut off, change the way we understand God and His forgiveness? Hint: Read 1 John 1:9 and identify the direct modifier (who or what receives the action) of the word forgive.

2. Why do you think that Jesus used the money analogy when teaching His disciples about forgiveness?

3. Why it is that the one forgiving holds all of the power in the relationship?

4. Why is forgiveness non-relational?

5. How does it affect you to think about Jesus assuming the weight of your unpaid debt in relation to the debt that you may hold over others?

6. Why is there a necessity for our heart belief to be pure when it comes to forgiving "seven times seventy?" Why does having lie-based heart belief make it difficult to forgive even one time?

7. If you are reading this book as a small group read out loud through the "Pause and Review" section above to review the basic concepts you have learned before looking at the principles of forgiveness in the chapters that follow.

# Chapter Five

## Principle One: Forgiveness requires that we assess the debt and take an account

*"And when he had begun to settle them [the accounts of the servants], there was brought to him one who owed him ten thousand talents"*
*(Matt. 18:24)*

The king called his servants to give an account of what was owed him. Assessing the debt or giving an account is the prerequisite for forgiveness. How are we to forgive a debt if we do not know what it is? People often try to forgive in generalities when they forgive the "debts" of others. They might pray and confess, "I choose to forgive my dad for *every* hurtful thing he ever did to me." However, all-encompassing confessions rarely have any specific impact. There are possibly cases where it proves successful, but based upon our experience, we believe it is rare.

I (Ed) am not personally aware of any case where this has been successful in nearly forty years of helping people through ministry. To be sure, I tried to lead many people to choose to forgive, to pray a prayer of confession and do the right thing (try to maintain the forgiveness), but genuine and lasting forgiveness did not seem to follow. Time always reveals whether true forgiveness has occurred or not. If any effort is required to maintain the "forgiveness" following choosing to forgive and praying the prayer, then forgiveness did not occur.

## What is the "Debt" That Needs to be Forgiven?

The debt (what we believe is owed us) appears to keep us in emotional bondage to the debtor. For as long as we hold the debt over the debtor's head, it seems we remain attached to him. This is true, but not in the way that we may think. What keeps us enmeshed with the debtor is not the actual monetary arrears that have gone unpaid. It is not what is owed us that causes our struggle in letting the debt go. Rather, it is due to three things:

1) how we have interpreted what happened to us at the hands of our debtor,
2) what we believe the outcome would be should we forgive, and
3) the "solutions" we have devised to avoid that outcome. This is where we need the truth from God's perspective, because our vantage point is lie-based and keeps us holding on to the debt.

## Heart Belief and Solution Belief

As a review of what we have already discussed, there are two different beliefs at play here. First there is our heart belief—that is, how we have interpreted what happened to us and why we believe it happened. This belief will be expressed as a statement of either our self-identity or our perceived state of being or condition. A self-identity belief can be something like, "I am worthless, a reject, defective, or unlovable," whereas a state-of-being belief might be something like "I am helpless, powerless, trapped, out of control, abandoned, dirty, or tainted."

The other type of belief at play here is what we refer to in TPM as a "solution belief." A solution belief motivates behavior and is designed to serve us in some fashion. It may be understood as either a protection from something or someone, or an expression of revenge to punish or hold a person accountable. Solution belief behavior is any behavior that serves us in some manner in relation to the debt that we harbor against someone. It is the belief that supports our solution to a perceived problem; such as, "If I forgive he will get by with what he did to me (the problem). By not forgiving I hold him accountable (solution belief)."

It may indeed be true that a person's actions were totally unjust, evil, and uncalled for. Again however, it is not this truth that makes us unwilling to forgive, but rather, our lie-based interpretation of what happened (heart belief) and what we believe may be the negative outcome of forgiving (the problem) culminating in our futile solutions. If the debt itself was the reason that we could not forgive, then there would be no hope of ever forgiving, since the debt will always remain. Forgiving a debt does not remove it, but only removes the responsibility for it from the one who held it. The loss remains.

### *There is a reason we have difficulty with forgiving.*

The reason we struggle with the idea of forgiving is always because of our lie-based perspective concerning the debt. When we know the truth with our hearts and can view the debt and the debtor from God's perspective we will forgive without hesitation. However, first we must deal with any lies that may be present and hindering forgiveness from occurring. The very fact that we are resistant to releasing a debt reveals we have a reason (based on a belief) for holding on to it. The problem is not the debt but rather the belief that keeps us from releasing it.

We believe lies with our heart that cause us to feel emotional pain. In order to manage this pain and contend with other perceived problems we develop what we have referred to as *solution beliefs*. Both our lie-based heart beliefs and our solution beliefs that hinder us forgiving will need to be replaced with the truth by His Spirit before forgiveness can occur.

In a TPM session when dealing with a *solution belief*, there are three questions we ask to help the person to identify his belief.

1) "If you were to consider forgiving the debt, would you sense any hesitation or resistance to doing so?" (This question exposes the presence of a lie-based belief.) If yes,

2) "What do you believe might happen if you were to forgive, that causes you to hesitate or resist forgiving?" (This question exposes the perceived problem.) Finally,

3) "What is your reason for not forgiving?" (This final question will usually reveal the belief that is keeping the person from genuinely forgiving, or the *solution belief.*) After asking these three questions the person should then be in position to hear from the Spirit and be persuaded of the truth.

### *There is a reason that we resist.*

As we have already mentioned, there are two types of belief that hinder us in forgiving: *heart belief* and *solution belief.* When we resist doing something, it is because we believe something about the consequence of doing it and because of the deeper emotional pain we harbor. The resistance is coming from what we believe would be the outcome of forgiving, and the deeper pain is flowing from the heart belief. In TPM we follow a prescribed protocol for helping a person to identify the lies they believe that hinder their knowing God's perspective.

The basic problem is always the same; people lack God's truth. When dealing with a heart belief, we first identify and connect with the emotion produced by such belief, then allow our minds to associate this emotion with any related memory. When the "right" memory surfaces there are specific questions we ask to help identify the belief causing the emotional pain. Once this lie is identified, it is offered to the Lord for His perspective. In this moment it is expected that the Spirit will *persuade* the person of the truth, releasing him of the lie he harbored. When the person knows the truth the emotion will change to match the truth.

The solution belief is identified in a somewhat different fashion. We do not have the person focus on what he is feeling, but rather ask the three "solution" questions. The third question will usually expose the solution belief. Once it is identified we ask the Lord for His perspective. When the person knows the truth, the solution will cease to be necessary. When both lie-based heart belief and solution beliefs are replaced with truth, forgiveness should follow.

### *Seeing with the "Eyes of Truth"*

Our lie-based beliefs keep us from freely forgiving the debts of our debtors. Only when the Spirit persuades us of the truth can we forgive from the heart. Forgiveness is effortless when God opens the "eyes of the heart" and we view the debt and debtor through the eyes of Christ. When our vision clears we will be free to forgive and release the debt. If we continue to hold on to our own understanding and interpretation of what happened and our belief about the consequence of forgiving, we will find it very difficult, if not impossible, to forgive from the heart.

Intellectual belief is easy to come by. Basically all we have to do is apply ourselves to learning it. However, heart belief of the truth is only obtainable when granted by the Spirit. Heart belief is believing the truth, in faith, with absolute certainty. Unless God persuades us (*peitho*) of the truth in our heart, we cannot believe other than with our intellect.

> *Unless God persuades us (peitho) of the truth in our heart, we cannot believe other than with our intellect.*

### What About the Debt?

Someone may say, "But the debt must be repaid! He owes me for what he did to me!" This may very well be the truth, but this is not the cause of our refusal to forgive. It is not the debt that is the problem.

It may be that what we remember about what happened in the event is the truth. It may be true that what occurred was evil, wrong and unjust, but this is not the reason we feel what we feel today, or why we refuse to forgive our offender. The person may indeed have been totally wrong in his behavior, and we are completely just in our appraisal of all that occurred. But, again, it is not this that holds us captive and prevents us from forgiving. It is what we believe, based upon the conclusions we came to, and the meaning we ascribed to all of it (coupled with any solution beliefs that we devised for solving the perceived consequences of letting the debtor off the hook) that has us bound.

It is imperative that both the lie-based heart belief and the solution belief be identified and brought into the light. We must look to the Lord to release us (*aphiemy*) from what we believe so we can be free. When the Lord *forgives* us (releases/aphiemy) of our false belief through His illumination of the truth, we are free to release/aphiemy the debts of those who have owed us.

After we identify what we believe (our interpretation) about the experience, as well as the belief we hold concerning the consequences of forgiving, we are in the right position to have our heart persuaded of the truth. Having obtained God's perspective of truth, we will be free and empowered to genuinely forgive.

### *It's NOT About the Money*

Some people reading this may react and say, "What about the king's money? He lost millions of dollars!" Even after genuine forgiveness has taken place, the tangible loss will still be there. When the king forgave the servant his debt, the servant walked free, but the loss remained. The king still did not have his money.

What keeps us emotionally enmeshed to those who have hurt us is not the memory of the injustice or even the tangible loss of property, but it is that we have interpreted the situation through all our lie-based beliefs. We lack the truth of God's perspective. If the actual loss was the reason for our inability to forgive, then we would never be able to do so, since the loss would continue to be a reality. The actual loss is not the problem even though it is never repaid. It is only our belief (interpretation) which holds us captive, and when this is transformed by truth, we are released.

We see this principle in the writings of the Apostles. Because they rightly interpreted their suffering, i.e., the unjust treatment they received because of the gospel, they could rejoice and exult. What the Apostles endured was unjust, unmerited, and without cause. They responded with joy. How could this be? They viewed the evil brought against them (the debt) as beneficial, and from this perspective they were not only willing to forgive, but also to rejoice.

> The Apostle Paul wrote, *"...we also exult in our tribulations, knowing that tribulation brings about perseverance; and perseverance, proven character; and proven character, hope..."* (Rom. 5:3-5).

> James the Apostle said it this way, *"Consider it all joy, my brethren, when you encounter various trials, knowing that the testing of your faith produces endurance..."* (James 1:2-4).

Paul expressed this concept in another place when he said, *"...we know that God causes all things to work together for good to those who love God, to those who are called according to His purpose… If God is for us, who is against us?"* (Rom. 8:28-29, 31).

Peter said it this way, *"In all this* [their suffering and persecution] *you greatly rejoice, though now for a little while you may have had to suffer grief in all kinds of trials. These have come so that the proven genuineness of your faith—of greater worth than gold, which perishes even though refined by fire—may result in praise, glory and honor when Jesus Christ is revealed…"* (1 Peter 1:6-8).

Jesus said this concerning persecution: *"Rejoice and be glad, for your reward in heaven is great, for in the same way they persecuted the prophets who were before you"* (Matt. 5:12).

### It all goes back to interpretation.

How can Jesus and the apostles tell us to exult in tribulations and consider it joyful when we are treated unfairly, unjustly, or persecuted? *Interpretation.* It really is all about how we interpret our experiences. *The degree to which we are able to view the actions of others from God's perspective is the degree to which we will walk in true peace and freedom after such experiences.* When we hold God's perspective, we are free to release those whom we have held indebted to us.

---

*THE DEGREE TO WHICH WE ARE ABLE TO VIEW THE ACTIONS OF OTHERS FROM GOD'S PERSPECTIVE IS THE DEGREE TO WHICH WE WILL WALK IN TRUE PEACE AND FREEDOM AFTER SUCH EXPERIENCES. WHEN WE HOLD GOD'S PERSPECTIVE, WE ARE FREE TO RELEASE THOSE WHOM WE HAVE HELD INDEBTED TO US.*

---

When we know the truth, it frees us. The key word found in these passages is "knowing." Knowing is believing. The "knowing" that frees us goes far beyond our intellectual understanding of it. This knowing is experiential and relational; it is heart belief. Again, heart belief is wholly accomplished by God as He persuades us of his truth. Intellectual understanding of the truth is something that any person can have whether a believer or unbeliever. Even the *"...demons believe and shudder"* (Ja. 2:19). However, heart belief cannot be accomplished by any person, only by God persuading us of the truth.

Paul said that he exalted in his tribulation because he "knew" that it was producing an eternal benefit; he held a heavenly interpretation of the events. James said to rejoice in our trials because the trial produces *"...endurance..."* and that endurance brings about a *"...perfect result..."* so that we *"...may be perfect and complete, lacking in nothing"* (Ja. 1:3-5). When we know this, we will rejoice.

It may indeed be true that others have hurt, robbed, mistreated, abused, and cheated us, running up an immeasurable amount of indebtedness. All of these things can be perceived to be a great loss. The Scriptures are clear that God has promised us an everlasting benefit that supersedes any loss we may have suffered. It says,

- *"God causes all things to work together for the good to those who love God, to those who are called according to His purpose...."* **(Rom. 8:28)**

- *"...if God is for us who can be against us..."* (Rom. 8:31)

- *"...momentary, light affliction is producing for us an eternal weight of glory far beyond all comparison..."* (2 Cor. 4:17).

- The Apostle Paul said concerning the great losses he suffered, *"...I count all things to be loss in view of the surpassing value of knowing Christ Jesus my Lord, for whom I have suffered the loss of all things, and count them but rubbish so that I may gain Christ..."* (Phil. 3:8).

So we see that our perception and interpretation of what is happening, or has happened to us, determines how we feel about it. If we view the actions of others against us as our loss and fail to see God's ability to use it for our benefit, we will become angry, bitter, and be unable to forgive. The truth remains that it is what we believe with our heart, not what has happened to us, that produces what we *feel*.

---

*WHAT WE BELIEVE WITH OUR HEART AND NOT WHAT HAS HAPPENED TO US, IS WHAT PRODUCES WHAT WE FEEL. WE FEEL WHAT WE BELIEVE. WHEN WE CAN VIEW OUR SITUATION THROUGH THE EYES OF CHRIST, FORGIVENESS WILL FOLLOW.*

---

### Trying Harder to Forgive Has Little Impact

Most of us already know, and intellectually believe, the truth about the benefits of forgiving. We know with our intellect that forgiving is the prudent and spiritual thing to do. However, believing with our intellect that we ought to forgive can be far removed from believing it with our hearts. Because of this, forgiving remains difficult for many of us. Some have tried very hard to believe the truth about forgiveness, thinking that a greater effort in mental application might be helpful. *However, our having to exert any effort to believe the truth is an indication that we already hold a different belief that is contrary* to it.

We need to believe the truth with the heart, but only God can grant this form of belief. Heart belief is the essence of faith, and faith is a gift from God. To know the truth with our heart, we need God to gra*nt us a "...Spirit of wisdom and revelation, so that [we] may know him be*tter*...," that "...the eyes of [our] heart[s] may be enlig*htened..." (Eph. 1:17-18). Unless God renews our mind with His truth, we will continue to focus on the debt and have great difficulty in forgiving *it*.

### *Holding People Accountable is Still Valid*

We are not denying that suffering a tangible loss is important, or painful, and it should be addressed when possible. People do need to be held accountable for their sin. If I owe the bank money, then I need to be responsible and repay it. I am not seeking to minimize the sins of others, but only to say it is not the debt that keeps us emotionally enmeshed with those who have hurt us. We are bound by what we believe, and this keeps us from forgiving. Our unwillingness or inability to forgive binds us emotionally to our offenders.

This enmeshment is not caused by what others did or did not do, but it is caused by what we believe about it. It is the lie-based heart belief as well as our futile solutions we hold that keeps us bound. We need the Spirit of truth to persuade us of His perspective. Thus, we can be freed without any involvement or cooperation from the ones who owe us. This is very good news!

## *Discussion Questions*

1. What is it that needs to be forgiven, the person or the "debt?" Explain your answer?

2. What is the difference between a heart belief and a solution belief? How do they work in tandem and why must they both be addressed before forgiveness can occur?

3. If the debt owed us is not what has us enmeshed with the person who hurt us, what has us bound and how might we find release?

4. How did Jesus and the apostles deal with the difficulties caused by their "debtors"? Hint: Read through these passages again. Rom. 5:3-5, James 1:2-4, Rom. 8:28-29, 31, 1 Peter 1:6-8, Matt. 5:12

5. Do you find it difficult to separate the offender and his offense? How is forgiving the debt different from forgiving the debtor?

*Chapter Five: Principle One: Forgiveness requires that we assess the debt and take an account*

# Chapter Six

## The Importance of Memory in Taking an Account

*"...the kingdom of heaven may be compared to a king who wished to settle accounts with his slaves." (Matt. 18:23)*

We cannot take an account of what is owed us without first remembering it. This is where memory plays a vital role in the process of forgiving. Memory provides us with a context in which we are better able to identify the debt as well as the lies that hinder our forgiving. When we remember what was done to us, we can better identify our interpretation (heart-belief) of this event. This in turn helps us to identify the current lie-based belief which is founded upon that interpretation. Our lie-based beliefs produce the emotional pain that helps keep us emotionally enmeshed with our debtor.

### *Memory is not our problem.*

I (Ed) have many childhood memories of my grandfather whom I called "Pawpaw." Many of them are good, but some are not so good. I have one particular memory of him being angry with me and chasing me around the yard. I believed that I was going to be hurt and that I was powerless to stop what was happening and therefore I felt immense fear. I have worked through this memory using TPM, and now, when I look at that same memory, there is no fear to be found, since the Spirit has replaced my lie-based heart belief with His perspective.

During the ministry session in which I first chose to revisit that memory, I did feel fearful. When I received the truth from the Spirit, all the fear dissipated. As strange as it may sound, the memory was never the reason for my feeling fearful. In fact, our memories themselves do not hold any feelings at all. A memory cannot produce a feeling any more than the photograph of my now deceased grandfather. It is just a picture.

The feelings I felt when I revisited this memory were not in the memory or because of the memory, but rather they came from the current belief (I am powerless) I had come to believe as a child. The moment I embraced the belief as a little boy, it became my current heart belief and remained ever present. The reason that memory felt painfully bad when I looked at it later, was because of the current belief through which I was viewing it, not because the memory itself produced bad feelings.

During the experience of being chased by my grandfather, I believed I was powerless to keep from being hurt. This belief remained after the fact and traveled along with me in real time from that point forward, along with thousands of other additional lies I accumulated. This belief became a lie-based heart belief which I harbored for most of my life, and through which I would interpret that memory and other similar life experiences.

### *Memory–or the record of an event–changes over time*

A memory morphs and even fades as it is remembered and replayed. Sometimes it merges with other memories, different elements are forgotten, and blanks are filled in. On the surface, it appears that the belief stays constant, as it is reinforced by our using it to interpret each new life experience and situation. However, I use not only that earlier belief, but also all that I currently hold as the "truth."

Does this mean memory cannot be trusted? I can't say with certainty. However, if it can't be trusted at all, then our criminal justice system is in big trouble. But this really doesn't matter since validating a memory isn't the purpose or intent of helping a person to identify the lies that he believes. Memories are not the problem and do not need to be verified in order for a person to find genuine and lasting freedom and eventually forgive.

If protocol is accurately followed during a TPM session, no "memory" that is reported should ever be surfaced by the facilitator suggesting anything or providing any opinion about what may or may not have occurred in the person's life. Any memory that is reported in a TPM session should always be the result of the person's own initiative and never because of the suggestions or promptings of the ministry facilitator.

---

*ANY MEMORY THAT IS REPORTED IN A **TPM** SESSION SHOULD ALWAYS BE THE RESULT OF THE PERSON'S OWN INITIATIVE AND NEVER BECAUSE OF THE SUGGESTIONS OR PROMPTINGS OF THE MINISTRY FACILITATOR.*

---

### *Interpretation determines how we feel and what we feel*

If we feel bad in a new life experience, it is because we are interpreting the new situation from our current heart belief. What we believe with our heart determines how we view each new life experience and, to a great extent forms our reality of things. When our current heart belief is renewed by God's truth, the memory will no longer trigger painful emotion, and our response to our current situation will also calm down. When we know the truth we will feel what the truth feels like as opposed to what the lie felt like. It is also because of our lie-based heart belief that we struggle when it comes to forgiving. Forgiveness will be difficult (if not impossible) as long as we hold belief that is contrary to forgiving. Unless our heart belief is made pure, and we are able to view our situation from God's perspective, our struggle to forgive will continue.

After we know the truth, although the memory and the current situation remain the same, neither will continue to feel as it did when it was being interpreted through the false belief. This is not suggesting that what happens in our current situation is not unjust or evil, since it very well may be. However, it is the way we interpret the situation—from heart belief—that will determine how we respond to it emotionally.

***Memory helps us answer the question: "How did I come to believe what I currently believe which is causing me to feel what I feel?"***

Our response to any given situation is the outcome of our minds associating what we perceive to be happening with something we have experienced before, which is now recorded as memory. When we remember what happened to us, we can also access the belief that we formed in the context of that earlier experience. This belief and not the memory itself, is the source of what we feel in the moment.

Heart belief was established in the context of the life event, but is not stored in our past. The memory does not contain our current belief, nor is the memory itself the reason we feel what we feel. We remember what happened (this is the memory), but we believe what we believe, in the present. Heart belief was formed in the earlier life event, but has become our current belief we are using to interpret our present situation. This is why we struggle with forgiving those who offend us day-to-day. Our early established heart belief is the lens for how we interpret what occurs moment-by-moment. Until we view life through the lens of truth, we will continually interpret things through darkened glasses.

---

*THE MEMORY DOES NOT CONTAIN OUR CURRENT BELIEF, NOR IS THE MEMORY ITSELF THE REASON WE FEEL WHAT WE FEEL. WE REMEMBER WHAT HAPPENED (THIS IS THE MEMORY), BUT WE BELIEVE WHAT WE BELIEVE, IN THE PRESENT.*

---

Again, the memory of the event where we established our heart belief helps us to discover the underlying belief we are still carrying. If we are unable to identify this, we will presume our present emotions are based upon what is occurring in our current situation and come to false conclusions. As long as this is the case, it is unlikely we will forgive.

Therefore, we often wrongly assess the current situation as being the cause of our emotions. For example, how many times have you said to your spouse or fellow worker, "You make me feel so …[emotion]!" In fact, however, nothing or no one can ever make us feel anything we may feel. We always feel what we believe. What our spouse or our fellow worker did toward us may indeed have been wrong and unjust, but our emotional reaction was based upon how we interpreted what they did. Our interpretation was based upon what we already believed before they did what they did. There is hope in this. God can renew our minds with truth, and thus, transform how we respond in any given situation.

As we have already illustrated, our beliefs are the glasses through which we interpret our current situations. Identifying the memory where we learned this belief provides us with the means to rightly identify what we currently believe as well as why we feel what we feel. Again, this concept is fully detailed within the TPM training.

By remembering what we believed to have happened as well as the conclusions we came to believe at the time of the event, we are enabled to "take an account" of the wrong done to us. We are also able to discover any "solution" we may have adopted at the time to deal with the perceived problems that the situation created for us.

---

*BY REMEMBERING WHAT WE BELIEVED TO HAVE HAPPENED AS WELL AS THE CONCLUSIONS WE CAME TO BELIEVE AT THE TIME OF THE EVENT, WE ARE ENABLED TO "TAKE AN ACCOUNT" OF THE WRONG DONE TO US. WE ARE ALSO ABLE TO DISCOVER ANY "SOLUTION" WE MAY HAVE ADOPTED AT THE TIME TO DEAL WITH THE PERCEIVED PROBLEMS THAT THE SITUATION CREATED FOR US.*

---

In TPM, we recognize "solutions" to be any behavior that has been employed to protect oneself from perceived pain, resolve an internal conflict, or keep something from happening that one may want to avoid. Whenever we erect a means for self-protection, we cut ourselves off from any hope of freedom.

The very "solution" we came up with to protect ourselves is the rope that keeps us moored to the dock of animosity and resentment. For example, I might come up with a solution that says, "If I ever forgive him, he will just get away with what he has done. (Perceived problem) Therefore, by not forgiving him, I am holding him accountable" (Solution belief). The perceived problem ("he might get away with what he did") is solved by not forgiving him and by "holding him accountable." However, this solution guarantees that we will never forgive, and thus be perpetually enmeshed with the one who offended us.

Or other reasoning, "If I forgive him, I will be hurt again (perceived problem). My anger toward him protects me" (solution belief). "If I forgive, then I am saying what he did was okay (perceived problem). By not forgiving, I am letting him know what he did was wrong" (solution belief).

The problem with the solutions we create to resolve our perceived problems is that they do not solve anything and actually keep us in bondage. The very solutions we hope will solve our problems, actually create more serious problems. Until we find freedom from the lies that motivate our solution behaviors, we will remain emotionally enmeshed to those we are refusing to forgive.

> *THE PROBLEM WITH THE SOLUTIONS WE CREATE TO RESOLVE OUR PERCEIVED PROBLEMS IS THAT THEY DO NOT SOLVE ANYTHING AND ACTUALLY KEEP US IN BONDAGE. THE VERY SOLUTIONS WE HOPE WILL SOLVE OUR PROBLEMS, ACTUALLY CREATE MORE SERIOUS PROBLEMS.*

### *The TPM PROCESS: A Tool for Identifying Lie-based Heart Belief*

In TPM we use what we call the Ministry Process. This process is a ministry tool, or system which consists of seven "boxes" each containing specific questions, which help us identify what it is we believe that is causing us to feel what we feel. In this context, we focus on what it feels like to consider forgiving a person for something. Where there is unwillingness to forgive, there will be the presence of negative emotion. Typically, this emotion will be one of the many members of the anger family: rage, bitterness, offense, irritation, resentment, hate, rancor, etc.

In TPM we recognize that negative emotions are our friends, pointing us in the direction we need to take in order to identify what we believe. Emotion is like a smoke trail leading back to the fire. Once the lie is identified, it can be offered to the Lord for His perspective. This is when the Spirit can persuade our hearts of the truth. When this occurs, forgiveness will naturally follow. When we believe the truth with our hearts, we can also "forgive from the heart".

Conversely, until the lie-based belief holding our resentment and anger is brought out into the light, no genuine forgiveness will come about. Unless the Lord replaces our lie-based perspective with one from His perfect vantage point, we will hold tightly to our resentment and not be able to forgive.

The good news is this: when we are willing to identify and expose our lie-based belief to the Lord, the Spirit will reveal His heavenly perspective concerning what happened. When we know this truth, and begin to view the person through the eyes of Christ, we will easily release the debt. We can expect forgiveness to be the natural outcome of our own freedom. When God frees us, we are then free to release others. However, we cannot forgive without first assessing and acknowledging what it is that we need to forgive. This is why we, as did the king, need to take an account of what is owed to us.

### *Healing Memories is Not Needed Here*

So, we see that if indeed the memory was the problem, we could not fix it. Memory cannot be changed or "healed." Memory is not the source of our pain and does not contain our current lie-based belief. It may well hold the memory of what we believed at the time of the life experience, but it does not contain the belief that is now producing the pain in our lives. Freedom does NOT come by "healing the memory", but by identifying the lie that we currently believe and then receiving the Lord's true perspective. When this occurs 'the glasses' fall off and the "eyes of our heart" are opened, so that we may see with clarity.

---

*FREEDOM DOES **NOT** COME BY "HEALING THE MEMORY", BUT BY IDENTIFYING THE LIE THAT WE CURRENTLY BELIEVE AND THEN RECEIVING THE LORD'S TRUE PERSPECTIVE.*

---

People who misunderstand this concept may mistakenly think the memory has the power to cause us to feel things. They typically approach the memory as something that needs to be healed or restored. Memories do not need healing since they are not broken or even wounded. They are simply what we remember. People can sometimes view the memory as almost "alive" and active. They refer to such memories as "painful" memories, when in fact the memory produces no pain in and of itself. The memory, like our current situations, trigger the lie-based pain we carry.

As we have stated many times, our lie-based belief is the problem. The lie-based heart belief that was established at the time of the event is not a memory. Unlike the memory of the event, the lie has traveled along with us through time and is ever present and always available to be used to interpret the next life situation. When we believe a lie within our hearts, the consequences will be much the same as if it were true. It is this lie-based heart belief that is at the root of our struggle to forgive.

Our heart belief not only dictates what we feel, it also wields great influence over our choices and behavior. Therefore, when we believe a lie, the outcome can be the same as though it were true. For example, if I believe that I am worthless, this belief will dictate how I live my life. I may be an underachiever because there would be no reason to try to be better, or I may go the opposite direction and overachieve to disprove my worthlessness. If I was abused sexually as a child and believe that I am dirty and shameful, I may resist sexual intimacy with my spouse because when I participate I feel badly about it.

Our beliefs shape our lives and conform us into their likeness. The Apostle Paul warned the church of Rome of this when he said, *"do not be conformed to this world, but be transformed by the renewing of your mind …"* (Rom. 12:2). When we know the truth within our hearts, it results in mind renewal and transformation. If we believe a lie, it will conform us into its definition.

What we currently believe with our heart is our current belief, not a part of any memory of what we believed at the time of the past experience. Because we understand that our heart belief produces the emotion we feel in any given circumstance, we are able to use this to help us identify which belief we are using to interpret the present moment. If we try to identify our heart belief through logic and reason while remaining focused on the present situation, we are unlikely to find our way. We need the original context where we learned the belief, in order to rightly understand how we came to believe what we believe.

This does not mean that we are looking for the belief in the memory, but only using the memory to help us understand how we came to our current beliefs. It is what we currently believe that is causing us to feel what we feel in the present. Without the earlier memory, we only have the present situation in which to find meaning for what we feel, thus we are likely to blame whomever is in the room at the time for our 'bad' feelings. The current life situation cannot answer the question, "How did I come to believe what I believe that is causing me to feel what I am feeling?" Without the earlier context—now our memory—we are limited in the way we can interpret the current situation. This is why we say things like, "You make me feel _____." This statement is not true, but does reflect how easy it is to come to a wrong conclusion when we lack accurate information.

Our heart belief—from which we operate—was basically in place by the time we reached our early teen years. We don't feel worthless and rejected today because our spouse complains about our actions or because our boss questions our work. Even if other people's motives are cruel, demeaning or unjust, their behavior is not the reason why we feel as we do. We feel bad because we are interpreting the moment through the belief we learned many years before and have carried forward as our current belief.

My current emotion is neurologically connected to the exact belief that needs to be replaced with truth. This belief is linked with every time and place where I used it to interpret life—especially the original point of entry. It is helpful to think of emotion as a smoke trail that is being produced by the fires of our lie-based heart beliefs. If you are trying to find the fire, follow the smoke trail.

# *Discussion Questions*

1. Why is memory not the problem when it comes to forgiving?

2. Why do we say things such as "painful memory", "wounded memory" or "traumatic memory" when describing the hurtful things that have been done to us? If the memory is indeed "painful, wounded, or traumatic" then how is it possible to come to a place where the memory no longer stirs up any painful feelings?

3. What is the problem with holding the view that memory needs to be healed?

4. Memory leads us to the answer of which important question?

5. Why do we need to know the answer to this question?

6. What might be the outcome of not knowing the right answer to this question?

7. If no person or situation in the present can cause us to have negative emotions, then why do we have them?

# Chapter Six: The Importance of Memory in Taking an Account

# Chapter Seven

## Principle Two: The one who "owes" us does not have the means to repay the debt.

### *"... He Did not Have the Means to Repay" (Matt. 18:25)*

The servant had a wife and children to support on a servant's wages. He did not have the means to repay the millions he owed the king. Let's do a simple calculation to see just how great his debt was:

The denarius was about one day's wage for a typical day laborer. This would be about 275-300 denarii a year, before taxes. A talent was a unit of measure close to twenty years of servant labor and this servant owed 10,000 talents! This means that after the first twenty years of labor, he would still owe 9,999 talents. This is also based upon him paying the king his whole paycheck. To pay back the full amount would require working about 150,000 years. In today's American terms, if the servant were earning $35,200 per year at minimum wage, his total debt would have been approximately $7,000,000,000.

The king took an account and quickly surmised that the servant was in way over his head. He knew there was no chance he would ever see this amount of money returned by the servant. Thus, repayment was not an option. The king realized that even in thousands of lifetimes, he could not repay such an enormous debt.

### *The One Who Hurts Us Cannot Repair the Damage*

It is common for emotionally wounded people, the mortgage holders, to look to the ones who have hurt them to "fix" or restore things and to make them feel better. This never works. Like the servant in the narrative, the ones who caused the pain do not have the means to repay. Only the Lord can address these lie-based wounds and take away the pain. The only remedy is freedom through God's truth.

---

*The ones who caused the pain do not have the means to repay. Only the Lord can address these lie-based wounds and take away the pain. The only remedy is freedom through God's truth.*

---

Too often we want the other person to either stop making us feel bad or make us feel better. The problem is he cannot do either. When we look to the offender for payment, restitution, or compensation, we will generally receive even more hurt. Even if others are made accountable for their sins, our freedom will not come simply because justice is served.

This is because it is not the person or his wrongdoing that is causing us to feel what we feel, but our interpretation of this experience; our own lie-based heart belief. What the person did may indeed have been unjust, but the resulting pain is not due to the person or the experience. Rather, what we are feeling is directly rooted in how we interpret what happened and why it happened, and our feelings are flowing from this lie-based heart belief. Once having embraced this lie-based heart belief, it becomes the lens through which we interpret life, also a driving force in our lives in many negative ways.

We are easily driven to seek acceptance, approval, love, and affirmation from others, especially from the very ones who have hurt us, in an attempt to have the debt repaid. Those who hurt us cannot pay back what they owe. Until we believe with the heart that the Lord has already met all of our needs (Phil. 4:19) and has *"...blessed us with every spiritual blessing in the heavenly places in Christ"* (Eph. 1:3), we will continue to look to others to fulfill us. This never works. We only feel needful or lacking because we do not know with our hearts the fullness that has been granted us in Christ. God *"... gave Him (Jesus) as head over all things to the church, which is His body, the fullness of Him who fills all in all" (Eph. 1:22-23).* Hearing the words, "Christ is all we need," may sound cliché, but nonetheless, it is the truth even if it does not feel true.

---

> *UNTIL WE BELIEVE WITH THE HEART THAT THE LORD HAS ALREADY MET ALL OF OUR NEEDS (PHIL. 4:19) AND HAS "...BLESSED US WITH EVERY SPIRITUAL BLESSING IN THE HEAVENLY PLACES IN CHRIST" (EPH. 1:3), WE WILL CONTINUE TO LOOK TO OTHERS TO FULFILL US. HEARING THE WORDS, "CHRIST IS ALL WE NEED," MAY SOUND CLICHÉ, BUT NONETHELESS, IT IS THE TRUTH EVEN IF IT DOES NOT FEEL TRUE.*

---

Conversely, our lie-based belief may cause us to totally reject and avoid a person who has hurt us, even to consider them as being dead to us. However, these actions have the very opposite effect to that which we intended. Our effort in this regard causes us to maintain our focus on the person. It takes much emotional energy to reject someone. The rejection of someone is not a onetime event, but a perpetual state of being. When we try to cut someone off we enter a perpetual cycle of cutting them off. We may live day-to-day without thinking about them, however, when we do encounter them or are reminded of them, the weight of our rejection of them again becomes apparent. Our attempt to cut a person off assures that we remain enmeshed with him. So, whether we look to this person to meet our wounded neediness or cut him completely out of our lives, we remain in bondage because of a debt we cannot forgive and which the person can never repay.

So, we see that the debt that others owe us is far too great for them to repay. Only the Lord can pay it back and restore the loss. God promises, *"... I will restore to you the years that the locust hath eaten, the cankerworm, and the caterpillar, and the palmerworm, my great army which I sent among you. And ye shall eat in plenty, and be satisfied, and praise the name of the Lord your God, that hath dealt wondrously with you: and My people shall never be ashamed"* (Joel 2:25-26, KJV).

### *All Needs Have Already Been Met*

The good news is, that according to the Scriptures, we do not have any needs that the Lord has not already met. If we are in Christ, then He is our all in all. We do not need Him to meet any additional need that we have; instead we need to come into the reality of what we already possess (Eph. 1:3).

Too often we look to others to meet the needs in our lives that have already been met by Christ. We are called to love and to bless one another, but not to meet those needs God has promised He has already meet. When we look to others to meet our innermost needs, we will eventually be disappointed.

### *Living in Community as Mature in Christ*

It is true that God created us to live in community, but not for the purpose of fulfilling each other needs. We are members of the Body of Christ, each one gifted in some special measure that compliments the other. However, God has promised to fulfill all of our needs according to *"His riches in glory..."* (Phil. 4:19) and *"...has blessed us with every spiritual blessing in the heavenly places in Christ..."* (Eph. 1:2) We are incapable of meeting these needs since they are already met, but rather, we are called to grow up in Christ and fulfill our role in accomplishing the mission of the Church while on the earth.

In a rather lengthy passage below we see how God has equipped His church by gifting His people to equip the Body for service. We see that Christ is our all in all making it possible for each of us to move toward maturity. God desires that we all grow up from out of our immaturity and neediness and learn to walk in the full stature of Christ.

> "...He gave some as apostles, and some as prophets, and some as evangelists, and some as pastors and teachers, for the equipping of the saints for the work of service, to the building up of the body of Christ; until we all attain to the unity of the faith, and of the knowledge of the Son of God, to a mature man, to the measure of the stature which belongs to the fullness of Christ. As a result, we are no longer to be children, tossed here and there by waves and carried about by every wind of doctrine, by the trickery of men, by craftiness in deceitful scheming; but speaking the truth in love, we are to grow up in all aspects into Him who is the head, even Christ, from whom the whole body, being fitted and held together by what every joint supplies, according to the proper working of each individual part, causes the growth of the body for the building up of itself in love..." (Eph. 4:11-16)

Neediness is not a Christian virtue but a common trait of children. Children are needy, therefore they are given parents. However, when we grow up and mature we are to "put away childish things..." (1 Cor. 13:11). We are called to grow up in Christ and learn to share in love, live in unity and bless one another since we all possess the fullness of Christ. Our feelings of neediness are not truth-based. When we think that we "need" someone to love us, be with us, admire us and care about us, we are not operating in the truth. If we truly understood how much God loves us and what God feels about us, these needy feelings would vanish.

To the degree that we discover our all-in-all in Christ, we will be become higher functioning members of Christ's Body. To the degree that we do not know the truth of who and what we are in Christ, we will be a drain on those around us from whom we are expecting our needs to be met. It is possible that some who read these words will react and resist hearing them. It is easy to take on the victim's role, complain about our hardship and look to others to rescue us. Until we are able to reframe our life situation as the refiner's fire purifying our faith, we will struggle. The Apostle Peter knew this about the believers when he warned them by saying,

> *"Beloved, do not be surprised at the fiery ordeal among you, which comes upon you for your testing, as though some strange thing were happening to you; but to the degree that you share the sufferings of Christ, keep on rejoicing, so that also at the revelation of His glory you may rejoice with exultation" (1 Pet. 4:12-13)*

No one likes to think of himself as being needy, but if needy is what we feel, then we do not know the truth. Rather than spending so much energy in trying to get others to love us, accept us, or not reject us, we might consider using these needy emotions to help us to identify the lies we believe that causes us to feel what we feel. The Spirit desires we know the truth and is willing to convince our hearts of it, if we will look to Him for it.

### *Looking to Others for that Which God Has Already Given*

Looking to others to fulfill us and meet some perceived need is commonly seen within the marriage relationship. We "fall in love" with a hope that the other party will fulfill us, meet our needs, satisfy our heart longings, only to be sorely disappointed. Only the Lord can fulfill us. We are called to bless one another, but the Lord is the only one who can meet our needs. Peter the Apostle said this concerning the marital relationship, *"...be harmonious, sympathetic, brotherly, kindhearted, and humble in spirit; not returning evil for evil or insult for insult, but giving a blessing instead; for you were called for the very purpose that you might inherit a blessing"* (1 Pet. 3:8-9).

The Scriptures clearly say, *"God will supply all your needs according to His riches in glory in Christ Jesus"* (Phil. 4:19), But until we know these blessed truths from the heart, we will keep looking in all the wrong places to have our needs met.

### *When the Truth Does Not Feel True*

The lie-based beliefs we hold in our hearts hinder us from knowing the reality of who we are in Christ and the fullness of His sufficiency. Until the Spirit persuades us of the truth, these lies will dictate how we view our needs and disappointment will follow. If we believe we are unloved, rejected, empty, overlooked, lacking, deprived, unimportant, and worthless, etc., we will be blinded to the truth and continue to look to others to fulfill us. The truth is that we are already made full in Christ whether this feels true or not. He has provided all we need of love, joy, peace, and all the fruit of the Spirit.

Some who read this statement might say, "That sounds nice, but it doesn't feel true." *When the truth doesn't feel true, it's because we believe something contrary to the truth, not because it isn't true.* This contrary belief fills the place in our heart that's intended to hold the truth. We cannot make a truth that we don't believe *feel true* by trying harder to believe it. Truth *feels* true when we believe it, and only the Spirit can bring this about. Only God can persuade us of the truth in our hearts.

When we look to others to fill some perceived, unmet need in our lives, we are chasing after the wind. Even if a person does meet what we believe is a need at that time, it cannot be sustained. At some point, they will fail us and we will feel needy again. We only feel needy because we believe we have a need to be met. We perceive those needs to be unmet, but when we hold a heavenly perspective, we will realize that Christ is our all in all and has met every need.

---

*IF WE BELIEVE WE ARE UNLOVED, REJECTED, EMPTY, OVERLOOKED, LACKING, DEPRIVED, UNIMPORTANT, AND WORTHLESS, ETC., WE WILL BE BLINDED TO THE TRUTH AND CONTINUE TO LOOK TO OTHERS TO FULFILL US.*

---

If we look to our debtor to restore something to us, meet some need, pay us back, or do anything to change what we feel, we will not get what we are looking for: *ever in this life.*

### *What about righteous indignation?*

Someone will surely ask, "What about righteous indignation?" I love the way we have our own Christian euphemisms for saying things. Righteous indignation is basically being angry without sinning. Nonetheless, being mad about something is still being mad. Anger is still anger. So, what shall we do about the anger we feel when we are unjustly treated? We will now turn our attention to dealing with anger: the most misunderstood emotion in the Christian community.

## *Discussion Questions*

1. Do you ever look to others to meet your needs? Do you believe that not having these needs met is the reason for what you are feeling? How do you respond to the idea that all of your needs have already been met in Christ?

2. It is common for us to perpetually attempt to gain approval, acceptance, or love from people who have failed us earlier in our lives. Why do you think we are prone to look to those who have hurt us to make us feel better?

3. According to the Scriptures, we do not have any needs that the Lord has not already met, since He has a*lready,* *"blessed us with every spiritual blessing in the heavenly places* in Christ" (Eph. 1:3). This being true, why do we ever feel like we are lacking and even look to others to meet our needs?

# Chapter Eight

## Principle Three: Anger is a normal reaction to injustice, but must be released before freedom will come.

*"But since he did not have the means to repay, his lord commanded him to be sold, along with his wife and children and all that he had, and repayment to be made" (Matt. 18:25)*

Our initial response to being wronged is typically to become angry, seek revenge, or demand justice. It appears the king reacted with anger when he came to realize the severity of the situation, because, he commanded the servant to be sold into slavery and even intended to send the man's wife and innocent children away with him. It seems that the king was very emotionally stirred, and rightfully so. If he was angry, then this anger was in response to a grave injustice.

Such anger was a normal, healthy response to this servant's irresponsible behavior. How he could have ended up so deeply in debt is difficult to comprehend. When the king saw the size of the debt, he knew that the millions owed him would not be returned. The right and just thing to do was to punish the servant. The king's initial reaction was justified and to be expected. However, he did not retain his anger or allow the *"sun to go down on his anger"* (Eph. 4:26). His forgiveness was not the result of anger, but rather of compassion. We will soon discover that until we have compassion, forgiveness will be unlikely to occur.

### *Anger Often Misunderstood*

Before moving on to compassion, it may be helpful to look a little closer at the king's angry response. Anger is probably the most misunderstood emotion dealt with by the Church community. Christians typically have little tolerance for anger. We are told that anger is sin and that mature, spiritual people do not get angry unless it is because of sin or injustice. Therefore, we learn to suppress anger when it arises.

This unfortunate indoctrination begins early when parents teach their children not to express anger. If a child is angry, he is scolded. By contrast, if a child is saddened, he is comforted, if he is afraid, he is consoled, and if he is worried, he is encouraged. However, if he is angry, he is in trouble.

In addition, anger may cause some to feel fearful when it is expressed by others. Those who grew up around adults with uncontrolled anger may have experienced hurt or chaos and, therefore, learned to avoid anger at all costs.

### *Permission to Be Angry*

The Bible tells us, *"Be angry, and yet do not sin; do not let the sun go down on your anger, and do not give the devil an opportunity"* (Eph. 4:26). Sinless anger sounds like an oxymoron. However, anger only becomes sin when it is held and allowed to fester or if it is acted out in an unrighteous manner. Paul tells us normal anger may become sinful if it is held on to for too long, allowing the devil an opportunity to influence us. God has designed us to react to injustice by feeling angry, but He then expects us to let it go quickly and operate from a different posture.

Injustice makes God angry, but only He can deal with it and express it with holy indignation. The Scriptures declare, *"...Never take your own revenge, beloved, but leave room for the wrath of God, for it is written, 'Vengeance is Mine,' says the Lord"* (Rom. 12:19). He will righteously pour His wrath on evil and bring about justice. It is easy to think there are times when our anger serves us well, but James the Apostle wrote that *"the anger of man does not accomplish the righteousness of God"* (Ja. 1:20). So then, we can be angry as long as we do not sin or hold on to it for very long. We also have to accept that all vengeance belongs to God and our anger cannot accomplish righteousness outcomes.

So what are you going to believe? Without any doubt *"...There is a way which seems right to a man, but its end is the way of death"* (Pro. 16:25). Even though we may feel that our anger is justified, acting on it is not the righteous path we should take. We really cannot get around the passage that clearly states that the *"...anger of man does not accomplish the righteousness of God."* (Ja. 1:20).

In Ephesians 4:26, the Apostle Paul gives us permission to be angry, but he then directs us to put anger away (Eph. 4:31, Col. 3:8). Despite appearances, there is no contradiction here. Paul was clear in his instructions. He said we can be angry if we do not sin or hold on to that anger. Anger can be a righteous emotional response to injustice, but feeling angry for a time and acting upon it are two different things.

In both Ephesians 4:31 and Colossians 3:8, Paul is referring to an anger the "sun has gone down upon," which has given Satan an "opportunity" and where sin has manifested within it. Whenever the devil is given opportunity, he always does the same thing: he deceives. The outcome of his deception leads to sin. For we know that *"...each one is tempted when he is carried away and enticed by his own lust. Then when lust has conceived, it gives birth to sin; and when sin is accomplished, it brings forth death"* (Ja. 1:14-16).

Satan is consistent in his behavior. Everything he does, he does with the intention to deceive hoping we will act out in a sinful manner. Even when he speaks the truth, his motive is to deceive. He *"...was a murderer from the beginning and has never stood for truth, since there is no truth in him. Whenever he tells a lie, he speaks in character, because he is a liar and the father of lies"* (Jo. 8:44).

---

> *Satan is consistent in his behavior. Everything he does, he does with the intention to deceive hoping we will act out in a sinful manner. Even when he speaks the truth, his motive is to deceive.*

---

Satan has a strategy here. When he finds us in a state of anger, he wants us to sin in it. The apostle Paul said, *"Be angry, just don't sin."* Satan's intent is that we "be angry" and sin. He also knows that if we will hold on to the anger after the "sun has gone down" we will be very prone to sin because of this anger. His strategy is to implant a belief in our heart that will cause us to hold on to the anger and carry it forward. He knows if he can succeed in getting us to hold on to the anger we will eventually sin. The lies he offers us to assure that we tighten our grip on the anger are beliefs such as, "Your anger will protect you from being hurt again," "Being angry holds that person accountable for what they did to you," "Anger provides you with some measure of control," etc. Once we embrace lies such as these, we will find it impossible to let go of the anger unless God persuades us of the truth. If it was true that our anger accomplished what these lies suggested, then it would be illogical to let the anger go.

When we are treated unjustly we should feel angry. But the next step is to recognize that we are also incapable of handling that anger righteously. Vengeance is the Lord's and He will repay. We must place the anger in His hands and rest in Him. If the "sun goes down" and we are still clutching that anger, we will be a target for the devil. If we embrace his lies, our anger will become fixed and it will be difficult for us not to continually act upon it. When this occurs Satan's mission is accomplished.

There is a cohort of sinful behaviors in which this form of anger is found: *"...bitterness, rage and anger, brawling and slander, along with every form of malice..."* (Eph. 4:26). No wonder Paul suggests expediency in dealing with our anger before we let the "sun go down." Yet in every case where we struggle to let anger go, there will be a lie holding it in place. We have learned in an earlier chapter that these forms of belief are referred to as "solution beliefs." Rather than trying to force ourselves to loosen our grip on the anger, it makes more sense to identify the belief that keeps us holding on to it so tightly.

### *Three Helpful Questions*

In TPM we deal with anger felt toward anyone or thing other than God by using the three questions found in the TPM SOLUTION Box. If you choose to take this training, the full explanation will be provided you. Here is a preview of those questions as they relate to the anger solution.

1) *"Do you feel any hesitation or resistance at the thought of letting your anger go?"*
2) *"What do you believe would happen if you did let it go, that causes you to hesitate or resist?"*
3) *"What is the reason for holding on to your anger?"*

The first question is designed to reveal the presence of lie-based beliefs that are holding the anger in place. It does this by identifying the presence of hesitation or resistance at the thought of letting the anger go. When we ask this question we are not asking the person to do anything with their anger, but only to look for any hesitation, resistance or "push back" at the thought of forgiving.

The second question reveals the problem that the anger is hoping to solve. What they believe would be the negative consequence of forgiving exposes the problem they are trying to solve with their anger. For example, a person might say, "If I let my anger go he will get by with what he did."

The last question is designed to expose the lie believed that is the reason for the person holding on to his anger. For example, he might say, "My anger holds him into account for what he did." Once the lie is exposed the person is in the position to receive God's perspective. (This process is explained in detail in the online training in TPM. www.transformationprayer.org)

### *Nothing Righteous is Accomplished by Anger.*

It is a common deception to believe that anger is useful for accomplishing something of lasting value. There is no denying that many social injustices have been confronted by angry people, but Scripture does not support anger as a method to fulfill God's will. Many people try to do good while being driven by anger, while some people are never moved to action unless they are angered by what they are trying to change. Nevertheless, this does not justify their angry actions from God's perspective. We are still left with the fact that *"the anger of man does not accomplish the righteousness of God"* (Ja. 1:20). So then, there must be a better way.

Anger can be a righteous, emotional response to injustice, but acting on that anger is not God's desire for us. We should "be angry" but then leave vengeance to the Lord. Jesus said, *"bless those who curse you, pray for those who mistreat you… love your enemies, and do good, and lend, expecting nothing in return; and your reward will be great, and you will be sons of the Highest; for He Himself is kind to ungrateful and evil men"* (Luke 6:28, 35). We are told to be angry at the injustice, defer it to God, and then act in love. Here again, just because this may not feel true to us does not mean that it is not the truth.

Once someone challenged me (Ed) in this thinking. He said to me, "The ministry I do is driven by my anger! It is because of the injustice done to me and the anger I still feel about it that I am compelled to defend the helpless and rescue the weak and powerless." I simply asked this person how he interpreted James 1:20 that says, *"... the anger of man does not achieve the righteousness of God"*? I followed this question by asking him, "Wouldn't having the *'...Peace of Christ* [to] *rule in your heart...'* (Col. 3:15) as the motivating force be better than being driven by anger?" He said he would need to think about it. His anger was serving a purpose for him, but I'm afraid it wasn't a righteous one.

If the sun goes down on our anger and Satan is afforded the opportunity, he may plant a "purpose" in our heart for retaining it. Once this is accomplished, it is nearly impossible to let the anger go, since we now harbor a lie-based reason for keeping it. Again, reasons such as, "My anger protects me," "My anger holds the one who hurt me accountable," "My anger keeps me in control," or "My anger empowers me to act," are common.

---

*IF THE SUN GOES DOWN ON OUR ANGER AND SATAN IS AFFORDED THE OPPORTUNITY, HE MAY PLANT A "PURPOSE" IN OUR HEART FOR RETAINING IT. ONCE THIS IS ACCOMPLISHED, IT IS NEARLY IMPOSSIBLE TO LET THE ANGER GO, SINCE WE NOW HARBOR A LIE-BASED REASON FOR KEEPING IT.*

---

The question I did not ask this man was why he still felt this anger after so many years. When the sun goes down on our anger and we continue to hold it, then the anger is no longer caused by what happened; it is now sustained by the lie that Satan had opportunity to plant in our hearts. The Scriptures are clear, *"be angry, and yet do not sin, do not let the sun go down on your anger, and do not give the devil an opportunity..."* (Eph. 4:25-26).

On another occasion someone reacted to me (Ed) saying, "Anyone would respond the way I did to what happened. What that person did was wrong and unjust! How else should I have felt?" I agreed with him that what he described was, in fact, bad and unacceptable. However, he did not agree with me when I pointed out to him that his emotional response was not based upon what had occurred, but on how he interpreted what had occurred.

When we say our negative reactions to the difficulties that come our way are justified and an expected response, then passages such as *"...if God is for us who can be against us..."* (Rom. 8:31) or *"...For momentary, light affliction is producing for us an eternal weight of glory far beyond all comparison..."* (2 Cor. 4:17) need to be reinterpreted.

What do we do with the Apostle Paul's perspective where he said,

*"... we also exult in our tribulations, knowing that tribulation brings about perseverance; and perseverance, proven character; and proven character, hope; and hope does not disappoint, because the love of God has been poured out within our hearts through the Holy Spirit who was given to us"* (Rom. 5:3-5)

or Jesus who said,

*"..."Blessed are you when people insult you and persecute you, and falsely say all kinds of evil against you because of Me. Rejoice and be glad, for your reward in heaven is great; for in the same way they persecuted the prophets who were before you"* (Matt. 5:11-12)?

### *Not Forgiving and Holding on to Anger*

The reason we are unwilling to forgive someone is because we believe something that opposes forgiveness. If you were to identify the emotions that accompany unforgiveness, you would be likely to find one or more members of the anger family. Anger held on to after the "sun has gone down" remains because of a lie. We may initially feel righteous anger in the context of an injustice, but once the "sun goes down" we remain angry because of something else. Our anger ceases to be about what happened (the debt) and becomes centered on self-protection, revenge, holding someone accountable, maintaining control, etc. So when dealing with unforgiveness or anger, the process is the same.

---

*WE MAY INITIALLY FEEL RIGHTEOUS ANGER IN THE CONTEXT OF AN INJUSTICE, BUT ONCE THE "SUN GOES DOWN" WE REMAIN ANGRY BECAUSE WE BELIEVE A LIE ABOUT LETTING IT GO.*

---

As I described in an earlier chapter, when someone came to me expressing anger/unforgiveness about something in years past, I would quote a few Bible verses about anger and eventually persuade them to confess their "anger sin," repent, and choose to forgive as an act of their will. Most would at least try to do this, since it seemed the prudent thing to do. They might even have felt better for a while, but in most cases, they would start showing signs they were still holding on to the debt, causing their bad feelings to linger.

As stated earlier, general and global prayers to let go of anger or try to forgive someone for "all they have done" will rarely work. For example, if a person believes the lie that forgiving will allow the one forgiven to get away with what he did, it is unlikely that forgiveness will occur. Likewise, if the person believes the lie that forgiving will leave him vulnerable to being hurt again, forgiving will be difficult. We are not likely to let go of our anger until we are free from the lies we believe that hinder us from doing so. And we will not forgive until we are free from the lies we believe that keep us from releasing the debt.

So, we see that if we hold onto anger for too long, we provide the devil an opportunity to deceive us into staying angry. He knows if we embrace the lies he provides, then releasing the anger becomes unlikely and sinning predictably follows. So, if we "*let the sun go down,*" we give Satan the opportunity to plant a seed (a lie) into the fertile soil of our anger, resulting in a predictable harvest of sinful behavior.

Since Satan cannot make us sin, he is always looking for a way to make it more enticing for us to choose sin on our own. He knows that if we will stay angry, we will eventually sin in our anger. God said we can be angry, but not sin. We are permitted to be angry, but only for a short amount of time (sundown). If we don't let the anger go, Satan will provide us a reason and purpose for holding on to it. When that happens, it is only a matter of time before we act it out.

---

*If we "let the sun go down," we give Satan the opportunity to plant a seed (a lie) into the fertile soil of our anger, resulting in a predictable harvest of sinful behavior.*

---

## *Discussion Questions*

1. Why do you think that we are quick to scold our children when they act out in anger, whereas, when they express negative emotions such as fear, worry, or anxiety, we respond with care and concern?

2. Why does the enemy want us to hold onto our anger? How does he convince us to do so?

3. Think of the last time that you felt angry. What was the situation that stirred you up? Can you identify the belief that caused you to hold onto your anger? Hint: It was not because of what happened to you.

4. Practice asking yourself the three TPM SOLUTION Box questions as it pertains to *your anger*.

    *"Do I feel any resistance or hesitancy at the thought of letting my anger go?"*

    *"What do I believe would happen if I did choose to release my anger, that is causing me to resist or hesitate releasing it?"*

5. *"What is my reason for holding on to the anger I feel?"* (The anger is serving us in some fashion. It is solving a perceived problem.)

6. This last question is designed to expose the lie-based belief that is the reason our anger remains. If this reason feels true, then it is believed to be true. If you are willing you can offer it to the Lord so that He may persuade your heart of the truth.

# Chapter Nine

## Principle Four: Forgiveness has Nothing to do with the Attitude or Cooperation of the One Being Forgiven

*"The slave therefore, falling down, prostrated himself before him, saying, 'Have patience with me, and I will repay you everything'"* (Matt. 18:26)

At first glance it seems that the servant has come to his senses and is truly sorry for what he has done, but something he said at that time revealed his true heart. When he promised the king, *"I will repay you everything... the entire seven billion! You know I am good for it."* This was a bold-faced lie. His words revealed a heart of deceit. He and the king both knew he could never repay his debt and had no intention of ever doing so. The fact he had run up such an enormous debt tells us that, due to his irresponsible behavior, he was a thief. In our own lives, confronting a person who has hurt us often results in the same type of response: deceit, excuses, denial, or false promises.

We will be sorely disappointed and not able to forgive if our forgiveness is contingent on the attitude and integrity of the one we are forgiving. We sometimes believe the person should be broken, contrite, and humbled before we can forgive. This is simply not so.

---

*WE WILL BE SORELY DISAPPOINTED AND NOT ABLE TO FORGIVE IF OUR FORGIVENESS IS CONTINGENT ON THE ATTITUDE AND INTEGRITY OF THE ONE WE ARE FORGIVING. WE SOMETIMES BELIEVE THE PERSON SHOULD BE BROKEN, CONTRITE, AND HUMBLED BEFORE WE CAN FORGIVE. THIS IS SIMPLY NOT SO. FORGIVENESS IS FOCUSED ON THE DEBT, NOT THE DEBTOR.*

---

### *Forgiveness is Focused on the Debt, not the Debtor.*

I have heard people say things such as *"When he comes to me and admits what he did was wrong, then I will forgive him."* The truth is, forgiveness has nothing to do with the actions or response of the person being forgiven. We can forgive something even after someone has died. The grave may remove the person, but it does not remove the debt we feel is still outstanding.

When John the Apostle wrote, *"If we confess our sins, He is faithful and just to forgive us our sins and to cleanse us from all unrighteousness"* (1 John 1:9), the focus of forgiveness was on the sin, not the sinner. The sin receives the action of the verb *forgive*. God releases (*aphiemy*) or cuts off the sin, not the sinner. We certainly do not want to pray "God forgive ME" since we do not want *aphiemy* —to be cut off. We want to pray, "God forgive my sin."

The good news is, when Jesus died on the cross He *"took our sins away"* and put them as far as the east is from the west (Ps. 103:12). John the Baptist declared this about Jesus when he said, *"Behold, the Lamb of God who takes away the sin of the world!"* (Jo. 1:29) Because they have been taken away, we can be reconciled to God, *"...we have been made holy through the sacrifice of the body of Jesus Christ once for all"* (Heb. 10:10). Praise be to God! The person who is still lost in sin ought to pray, "God forgive my sin," but not, "God forgive me." He does not want God to "cut" him off, but he does want God to take away his sin and release him from his debt. Here again, it is possible that Jesus used the analogy of money because He wanted to draw a necessary distinction between the *debt* and the *debtor*.

---

*THE GOOD NEWS IS, WHEN JESUS DIED ON THE CROSS HE "TOOK OUR SINS AWAY" AND PUT THEM AS FAR AS THE EAST IS FROM THE WEST (PS. 103:12). JOHN THE BAPTIST DECLARED THIS ABOUT JESUS WHEN HE SAID, "BEHOLD, THE LAMB OF GOD WHO TAKES AWAY THE SIN OF THE WORLD!" (JO. 1:29)*

---

This is because when we forgive, we are not forgiving the person who has hurt us, but rather we are forgiving what was done (or not done) that has created the rift between us. Had the person not done (or neglected to do) something, we would not be feeling what we are feeling toward him. We are forgiving the deed and not the deed doer. We are cutting off (*aphiemy*) the debt, not the debtor. Later we will discover that unless the debtor himself seeks reconciliation (and meets specific criteria for bringing it about) he is already cut off from us relationally, since he has chosen to cut himself off from us.

### *The Anger Family*

Typically, what we feel when we haven't forgiven a debt is an emotion found in the "anger family." Anger has many relatives which include resentment, irritation, offense, rage, wrath, bitterness, sarcasm, indignation, belligerence, aggravation, fury, annoyance, exasperation, antagonism, and rancor. We typically feel emotions such as these when we hold a debt.

These emotions are associated with the "solution" we have established to deal with the perceived problem the person's offense has created for us. We have learned that these solutions are typically the "purpose" or reason that the enemy planted in our hearts. This purpose or lie-based belief was planted because we afforded the enemy "opportunity" by holding onto our anger after the "sun had gone down." Our present unwillingness to forgive is all tied into these varieties of anger and the solution beliefs we hold.

For example, Tom is angry with his father for abandoning him as a little boy. Tom interpreted his father's leaving him as an indication that he had no value. This heart-belief of worthlessness causes Tom to feel badly every time this belief is triggered. Tom discovered that being angry with his father was a solution, a way of protecting himself from this unpleasant emotion. Rather than feeling worthless, his anger would surface, covering up the worthless feelings. So now when Tom thinks about his father, all he feels is anger and an unwillingness to forgive. For Tom to forgive his father's debt would leave him holding his feelings of worthlessness.

However, when anyone else triggers this lie that Tom believes (that he is worthless) his anger is felt toward that person as well. The belief behind Tom's anger is "My anger protects me from feeling worthless." When someone does something that touches this belief, he feels worthless. However, almost instantaneous with the worthless feeling comes his protective feeling of anger. Unless Tom finds freedom from the lie of "worthlessness" and his anger solution, he will remain trapped in this perpetual cycle.

### When the Money Debt is Resolved and the Pain Remains

At the end of the day, if we had money taken from us, we may legally write off the debt and release the borrower of his obligation. The money debt is resolved, but how are we feeling? Do we feel free? Is the peace of Christ "*ruling in our hearts*" (Col. 3:15)? Do we feel compassion for the one who took from us? If not, then have we truly forgiven? We forgave the financial obligation, but a lie-based belief remains which holds us captive, causing us to feel what we feel. Therefore, it is the beliefs we harbor—both lie-based heart beliefs and solution beliefs—which are the real problem, even though the physical debt has been released. We need God to release us from what has us bound so that we can, in turn, "*forgive our debtors*" (Matthew 6:12).

Someone might still say, "Forgiveness is a deliberate conscious choice to be obedient to what the Bible teaches and what we may feel about it does not matter. We should just do the right thing and not pay attention to what we feel." This sounds noble, but it simply does not work. There is a reason we still feel badly after having "chosen to forgive." Because we feel whatever we believe, our negative emotional state is a symptom that we still believe a lie in our heart. When we know the truth in our hearts, and can view our debtor through the "eyes of our heart," we can forgive. Forgiveness is not a difficult task when we know the truth. When we are operating in the truth, forgiveness is an expected outcome, as is all the fruit of the Spirit.

---

*FORGIVENESS IS NOT A DIFFICULT TASK WHEN WE KNOW THE TRUTH. WHEN WE ARE OPERATING IN THE TRUTH, FORGIVENESS IS AN EXPECTED OUTCOME, AS IS ALL THE FRUIT OF THE SPIRIT.*

---

### Forgiveness is not dependent upon the debtor.

We see that forgiveness is not dependent upon any change in the one whose debt is being forgiven. His attitude, his participation, or even his behavior afterwards has nothing to do with our forgiving. We can be freed from the emotional entanglement when we experience the Lord's truth. Since it is only "what we have believed" that has entwined us with the one who owes us, simply knowing God's truth is enough to release us to forgive. When we know the truth that frees us from the lies that keep us holding onto our anger and unforgiveness, we will instantaneously feel differently toward those with whom we have harbored resentment. Only God can bring this about. We cannot simply choose to forgive as an act of our will. We need God to free us from the "snare" that holds us captive, so we may release the debt of the debtor.

### *This is Grace.*

God the Father looked past the sinner and forgave the debt. This is the meaning of true grace. This is what we need from God and what He does for us; He looks past the sinner and forgives the sin. Again, we hear the message of John the Baptist who declared, *"…Behold, the Lamb of God who takes away the sin of the world!"* (John 1:29). When Jesus died on the cross, his blood did not *cover* our sins like the blood of lambs and oxen did under the old covenant (Heb. 9). Rather, Jesus took our sins away—*aphiemy*—released us from our sins! *"If we confess our sins, He is faithful and just to forgive us (take our sins away) our sins…"* (1 Jo. 1:9).

## *Discussion Questions*

1. Does the attitude or lack of integrity of the one we are forgiving matter when it comes to our forgiving them?

2. What if they do not want us to forgive them and continue to do hurtful things? How might this impact our forgiveness?

3. Why do we need to forgive the "deed" as opposed to the "doer?" How are our lie-based beliefs related to forgiving the deed?

4. With which members of the "Anger Family" are you most acquainted?

5. What is the fundamental difference between the "forgiveness" of the Old Testament through animal sacrifices and what the death of Jesus accomplished? (See Hebrews 10:1-8)

# Chapter Ten

## Principle Five: Genuine forgiveness requires that we have compassion

*"[The king] ...felt compassion and released him and forgave him the debt..."*

The key to genuine forgiveness is compassion. When we continue to hold onto the lie-based beliefs that cause us to be angry and resentful toward a person, compassion will be elusive and true forgiveness will be difficult. Unless we can genuinely view the one who owes us a debt through a heart of compassion, it's unlikely that we will be able to forgive him. This is how the king in the story could relinquish such an enormous debt. *"And the lord of that slave felt compassion and released him and forgave him the debt"* (Matt. 18:27).

**Compassion is NOT something we muster up at will.**

We either have compassion or we do not. When we think about the person we need to forgive and the debt he owes, the feelings we have in that moment reveal much. If we feel the peace of Christ and compassion for the one who hurt us, then we are operating in truth, the Spirit's fruit is evident, and forgiveness has occurred. If we feel a negative emotion and an unwillingness to let the debt go, then a lie-based belief is present, and we are not free.

Someone might say, "Wait! What he did to me was wrong and unjust! He should pay!" This may be true, but it has nothing to do with forgiving. Forgiving is knowing the truth and acting in love. We cannot get to this place apart from a work of the Spirit.

---

*COMPASSION AND FORGIVENESS ARE NATURAL EXPRESSIONS OF A TRANSFORMED LIFE, NOT QUALITIES WE CAN PRODUCE OURSELVES. THEY ARE THE OUTCOME OF THE FREEING WORK THAT GOD HAS ACCOMPLISHED WITHIN US. ALTHOUGH COMPASSION IS NOT DIRECTLY LISTED IN GALATIANS 5:22 AS A "FRUIT OF THE SPIRIT," IT IS SERIOUSLY IMPLIED. AND SINCE IT CAN ONLY COME ABOUT IF GOD PRODUCES IT, IT IS HIS FRUIT.*

---

If we do not have compassion, there is a reason. Compassion flows freely and without effort because of knowing and being transformed by God's truth in our hearts, as does all the fruit of His Spirit.

### *What if sin is the problem?*

It's possible that sin may be hindering our ability to forgive. However, if this is so, then if we deal with the sin (in whatever manner our theology dictates), forgiveness should follow. If we deal with the sin and the forgiveness does not come, then there's obviously something else operating. If we have done this and forgiveness continues to elude us, and we also feel no compassion, then we might want to consider the possibility that other problems remain. We often assume that sin is the reason for all our bad behavior, and this may be so, but there are other factors at play that culminate in our behavior. What we believe has a major bearing on what we do or do not do. This is very true in the area of forgiveness.

If what we believe is a lie, it will cause us pain, typically masked by anger. Yet if we are willing to follow our pain to its true source—our lie-based belief—and receive God's truth, the pain produced by the wrong belief will dissipate. We will know the truth and will be free from the lies that were causing us our emotional pain. As a result, we will have peace and compassion, and the ability to freely release the debt. *Forgiveness is not something we have to try to do. It is what happens when we receive God's perspective and we ourselves are set free.*

---

*FORGIVENESS IS NOT SOMETHING WE HAVE TO TRY TO DO. IT IS WHAT HAPPENS WHEN WE RECEIVE GOD'S PERSPECTIVE AND WE OURSELVES ARE SET FREE. THE REASON WE STRUGGLE IN TRYING TO FORGIVE IS BECAUSE WE ARE GOING AGAINST OUR OWN HEART BELIEF. WE NEED THE SPIRIT TO PERSUADE US OF HIS PERSPECTIVE, SO WE CAN LET GO OF OUR OWN.*

---

### *False Humility and Promises*

In Matthew 18:26, the servant knew his time was up and fell at the feet of the king, pouring out lies and false promises. "I will repay it all…" Was the king taken in by this gushy show of false remorse? No. He saw his servant's pitiful state. He saw past the false promises to only two options: throw the man in jail or offer compassion. He chose compassion.

This not only revealed the heart of the king, but it also showed compassion to be the right response, even though the servant was unworthy. We too, will experience compassion for those who have hurt us when we know the truth from the Lord's perspective. Compassion will follow our own freedom, and when we feel compassion we will forgive effortlessly. *The reason we struggle in trying to forgive is because we are going against our own heart belief. We need the Spirit to persuade us of His perspective, so we can let go of our own.*

When we have the freedom that knowing the truth brings, we can be gracious and express compassion toward another who has hurt us. When God releases us (*aphiemy*) from our own lies, we are then free to forgive another's debt. When we come into truth and receive God's grace and forgiveness, we can more easily view the person who has hurt us from God's perspective.

### *Jesus felt what the truth felt like; always.*

The Lord experienced various emotions throughout the experience of his crucifixion. However, these were all based upon the truth and not lies. Jesus was responding from the truth He knew with His heart and His emotions corresponded to that truth throughout the entire ordeal.

Jesus revealed a portion of the truth by which He was operating immediately after one of His followers cut off the ear of one amongst those who came to arrest Him. Jesus healed the man's wound, then told his zealous follower to put his sword away. He explained why his action was unnecessary by asking the bewildered follower, *"...do you think that I cannot appeal to My Father, and He will at once put at My disposal more than twelve legions of angels?"* (Matt. 26:53). This was the truth based heart belief that Jesus had.

Because He knew the truth with His heart, Jesus was not feeling any fear, worry or anxiety. He knew that He could stop all that was occurring at any time by simply asking the Father to intervene. Everything that happened to Him occurred only because he was willing to endure it. Because Jesus knew the truth He felt what He felt and did what He did.

His emotions continued to reflect the truth of His belief when He expressed concern for His mother and asked John to watch over her. He also demonstrated care and interest towards the thief hanging next to Him, inviting him to share in Paradise. He expressed great compassion for the very people who had crucified Him when He prayed, *"Father forgive them, for they know not what they do..."* (Luke 23:34).

There is nothing in the crucifixion narrative to suggest that Jesus ever felt fear, anxiety, worry, helplessness, or powerlessness during this time. Jesus knew the truth and it was made manifest in how He responded to life around Him. It is only recorded twice that Jesus felt a negative emotion and on each occasion, he expressed the truth of what he was feeling. Although if it was negative, what He was feeling was from the truth He knew. While praying in the Garden He was filled with anguish *over the truth* that was set before Him. It was the truth that His Father was asking Him to suffer physical torture beyond imagination as well as making *"...Him who knew no sin to be sin on our behalf, so that we might become the righteousness of God in Him"* (2 Cor. 5:21) We have no idea what it may have felt to be perfected holiness and yet be asked to *"be sin"*, but this was what was before Him as He agonized considering it. However, it was also *"... because of the joy set before Him that He endured the cross..."* (Heb. 12:2).

---

*THERE IS NOTHING IN THE CRUCIFIXION NARRATIVE TO SUGGEST THAT JESUS EVER FELT FEAR, ANXIETY, WORRY, HELPLESSNESS, OR POWERLESSNESS DURING THIS TIME. JESUS KNEW THE TRUTH AND IT WAS MADE MANIFEST IN HOW HE RESPONDED TO LIFE AROUND HIM.*

---

While on the cross, Jesus cried out, *"My God, why hast thou forsaken me?"* (Matt. 27:46). This was when the Father looked away as Jesus took on the sin of the world. Again, the emotion He felt in this moment was appropriate for the truth. The good news is that because Jesus was abandoned, we will never be forsaken by God, so we will never need to feel what Jesus felt on that terrible day.

Jesus lived His life from truth and experienced emotions that corresponded with the truth that He believed. His circumstances did not dictate what He felt, but rather the truth that was resident within His heart was the very source of His emotions. The same is true for us, and we will always feel whatever we believe with our hearts (whether it is the truth or a lie). When we are feeling fearful, worried, stressed, anxious, helpless, powerless, hopeless, abandoned, unloved, or worthless, it is because of our lie-based heart belief and not because of our circumstances.

The truth produces emotions such as peace, joy, assurance, confidence and contentment. God desires that the *"peace of Christ rule[s] in our hearts,"* (Col. 3:15), but our lie-based heart belief can prevent this becoming a reality.

The Scriptures declare that the Lord Himself stands ready to grant us peace in every circumstance when we are in position to receive it, *"…may the Lord of peace Himself continually grant you peace in every circumstance"* (2 Thess. 3:16). Based upon this passage alone, we can be assured that our life situations do not keep us from His peace, but rather what hinders us from knowing His peace is our perspective and interpretation of them.

If we do not have peace in every circumstance, we should ask ourselves, "Why not?" If we do not experience the peace that Jesus Himself offers us, it is not because it is not available to us. Something is keeping it from being realized. God's truth will always produce His peace. If we are not experiencing God's peace, then we need to question if our beliefs line up with God's truth.

Jesus is our standard and example to follow. However, mimicking Jesus' behavior and endeavoring to try to feel differently than we do will not benefit us. His standard is *not* attained by effort, but by faith, or heart belief. Jesus completely believed the truth with His heart. He walked in a perfected faith. It is because Jesus believed His Father and trusted His direction that He felt what

He felt, and did what He did. Because Jesus knew and walked in the truth, He continually experienced peace.

---

*IT IS ONLY AS THE SPIRIT CONVINCES US OF THE TRUTH THAT WE CAN BELIEVE IT WITH OUR HEARTS. THIS IS FAITH: BEING PERSUADED BY THE SPIRIT OF THE TRUTH IN OUR HEARTS AND BELIEVING IT WITH ABSOLUTE CERTAINTY.*

---

Peter the Apostle described the Lord's response to the events of His crucifixion when he said, *"...since Christ also suffered for you, leaving you an example for you to follow in His steps, who committed no sin, nor was any deceit found in His mouth; and while being reviled, He did not revile in return; while suffering, He uttered no threats, but kept entrusting Himself to Him who judges righteously; and He Himself bore our sins in His body on the cross, so that we might die to sin and live to righteousness; for by His wounds you were healed"* (1 Pet. 2:21-24).

Jesus understood the purpose of the cross, and thus He endured it with joy. He was able to look out over the same crowd that had put Him on the cross and view them through the eyes of truth, feel compassion for them, and ask His Father to forgive them because they did not know what they were doing. We too can forgive when we know the truth in our hearts as Jesus did.

### *Faith: Believing the truth with the heart with an absolute certainty*

The fruits of the Spirit are made manifest when we know the truth experientially within our hearts, which is the essence of faith. This faith is unshakable, immovable, assured, and unwavering. For example, when God says He will supply all your needs, but this does not *feel* true to you, you are not believing it in your heart. Whatever you believe in your heart will also feel true. We feel whatever we believe. Someone will probably say, "We need to believe the truth whether it feels true or not!" This sounds noble and spiritual, but really doesn't make any sense and is putting feeling and belief in the wrong order. If we believe something, it will feel true. If what we say we believe does not feel true, we can be sure something is wrong.

---

*THE FRUITS OF THE SPIRIT ARE MADE MANIFEST WHEN WE KNOW THE TRUTH EXPERIENTIALLY WITHIN OUR HEARTS, WHICH IS THE ESSENCE OF FAITH. THIS FAITH IS UNSHAKABLE, IMMOVABLE, ASSURED, AND UNWAVERING.*

---

However, when the Spirit grants us the truth and we are able to view the one who owes us something through the eyes of Christ, we will have compassion. From this we will be able to release the person from the debt without any effort. This is only possible when the Spirit grants us the truth by "opening the eyes of our heart."

### *Genuine compassion is a wonderful gift to be shared*

Sharon and I (Ed) had been married about 10 years when the Lord blessed us with our first child. Sarah was a delightful child with an effervescent personality that could win over anyone's heart. This blessing came to a tragic end when little Sarah developed an undetected brain hemorrhage. She survived three brain surgeries, but eventually lost her fight for life and the Lord took her home. Sharon and I entered the darkest time of our lives as we grieved the loss of our little girl. At this time Sharon was five months pregnant with our son Joshua (co-author).

Before Sarah died, I had counseled people who came to me with different issues and losses. Now and then someone would come who had suffered the loss of a loved one. I would say, *"I know how you feel"*, or other pat answers. The truth is, I did not know how they felt, because I had not experienced anything like what they were experiencing. I could offer sympathy, but not *compassion*. Sympathy says, *"I feel sorry for you"*. Compassion says, *"I know the pain you carry, for I, too, have carried a similar burden"*.

Compassion can come alongside and encourage the one in pain, in a way that nothing else can. This is only possible because the one with compassion has been where the person is and he personally knows the pain. Many people tried to console me through my grief with their sympathy—and I appreciated it. Occasionally someone came and said, *"I know what you feel. I too, had a child who died."* When this happened, something inside of me reached out and grabbed hold of that person's words of encouragement. This person knew the pain of what I was feeling and could offer me true compassion.

Genuine compassion is a wonderful gift to be shared. It allows us to truly *"weep with those who weep."* (Rom. 12:15) and to *"…comfort those who are in any affliction with the comfort with which we ourselves are comforted by God."* (2 Cor. 1:4) Whereas, sympathy only goes so far. Sympathy can say, "I am sorry for your situation," but it cannot say, "I know how you feel." It allows us to show pity for a person's plight, but it is not compassion. People may appreciate sympathy, but genuine compassion will bring hope encouragement like nothing else.

### *When our "compassion" is something else*

In TPM we recognize that not all that we might call compassion is actually compassion. To clarify, the pain we are referring to here that merits compassion or sympathy is truth-based pain as opposed to lie-based. When people are experiencing truth-based pain then we should "weep with those who weep…" However, there is no need to express compassion or even sympathy for a person's lie-based pain since it is based upon a lie and not the truth. Rather, we should rejoice that they have identified the lies in their lives that is causing them to feel what they are feeling and that they are potentially very close to finding freedom.

Nevertheless, it is common for a ministry facilitator to feel badly when he witnesses the person agonizing through lie-based pain. The facilitator may assume that what he is feeling is compassion or sympathy when in fact, he is feeling something else.

A ministry facilitator may think that what he feels is compassion when in fact he has been triggered by his own lie-based pain. I have witnessed this occurring many times through the years when I present a live TPM training. During the training I often asked for a volunteer who was willing to allow me to demonstrate the TPM process by praying with them in front of the entire group. Without fail, when the person begins to work through a memory and starts expressing their emotional pain, (often by crying and sometimes even wailing,) many of the people in the group become very stirred emotionally, themselves, by what is happening. Many people will look down at the floor, look at their cell phones, some even leave the room. Then the facial tissues start being passed around in abundance. After the ministry session is over, someone will usually ask a question that reflects the issue of "compassion." It might be worded something like, "What are we to do during a ministry session when our compassion for the person wells up in us?" They may go on to explain that watching a person process such pain can be very difficult.

The truth is, what the other trainees were feeling was probably not actually compassion, but was their own lie-based pain being triggered by their witnessing the emotional pain of the prayer recipient. People will often resist this idea and say it is only natural to empathize when people are experiencing such pain. I try to graciously point out that, if we had been there when it happened, it would have been appropriate to feel something toward the person. However, the pain being expressed in the demonstration session is no longer related to what happened, but only to the person's current lie-based core belief. If anything, they should feel excited and joyful that the person is moving toward truth and freedom. Pain is a necessary part of that process.

If you find yourself feeling painful emotions while ministering with someone, you will do well to look and see why. You cannot answer this question with your logical mind, but rather you must feel your way there. Focus on your "compassion" and allow your mind to connect you with the memory of where you felt this same way before. Do not be surprised to discover that your compassion is actually something else.

# *Discussion Questions*

1. If compassion is not something that we can muster up ourselves, how do we obtain it? What might be hindering us from having it?

2. Why is compassion an essential element of forgiveness?

3. Why was it possible for Jesus to endure the cross with "...the joy set before Him?" Why was there no resentment, anger, or offense expressed by Him in this dark hour? What are we to learn from this?

4. What does it mean for God to "... open the eyes of our hearts?" How does this relate to compassion?

5. What do you feel when you encounter someone who is expressing emotional pain? It is possible that what you feel is genuine compassion for the other person's situation. However, it is also possible that what you feel is not compassion, but rather your own lie-based pain being triggered by hearing the other person's story. How can you determine the true cause of your feelings?

*Chapter Ten: Principle Five: Genuine forgiveness requires that we have compassion*

# Chapter Eleven

## Principle Six: Forgiveness emotionally releases the one offering the forgiveness, but may have no impact on the one whose debt is cleared.

*The king "released him and forgave him the debt, but that slave went out and found one of his fellow slaves who owed him a hundred denarii; and he seized him" (Matt. 18:27-28)*

Forgiving a person his debt does not guarantee that the person will repent or change. Notice the two contrasting words in this verse: *released* and *seized*. Here you see the true beneficiary of forgiveness: the king. When the king *released* the servant, he was freed from the anger and stress of maintaining the record. *So we see that forgiveness does NOT have the power to change the one being forgiven, but it can change the one who is doing the forgiving.*

The servant, on the other hand, although forgiven, was still in bondage to his lie-based thinking and *seized* his fellow worker. Only God can change people, and He will do so only if they want to change. Of course, there is always the possibility that our forgiveness might have a positive impact on the offender and motivate him to seek his own freedom in Christ. However, we have no guarantee that this will be the case and, therefore, this should not be our motive for forgiving.

It is good news that we can be emotionally free from other people and their behavior, whether they change or not. Other people's behavior does not have the power to control us emotionally, but our own belief does. Even if we forgave our offender "seven times seventy", this would still not guarantee the person would change, and we would be back where we started—unless we find freedom from the lies we believe that entangle us with the offender.

When we are willing to take ownership for the lies we believe and look to Christ, He will exchange our lie-based heart belief for His truth and replace our pain with perfect peace. When this occurs, it will not require any effort to release the one who wounded us. We will no longer have any expectations that our offender will change or will repay the debt and, instead, compassion for him will flow from our heart.

---

*When we are willing to take ownership for the lies we believe and look to Christ, He will exchange our lie-based heart belief for His truth and replace our pain with perfect peace. When this occurs, it will not require any effort to release the one who wounded us.*

---

### Forgiveness Releases the One Forgiving.

I (Ed) spent many years using TPM with a group of women who were all survivors of childhood sexual abuse. Each of these women had suffered unjustly as a child, and all of them had perpetrators who were in "debt" to them. Their innocence was stolen and their childhoods were twisted and confused. However, the truth about what happened to them was not the source of the pain they carried. In every case, their difficulty in forgiving was rooted in heart beliefs such as, "What he did made me dirty," "I am violated," "He stole what God intended for me," "I am damaged goods," and "I am worthless."

Not only did the women embrace heart beliefs in the trauma such as, "I am dirty and shameful," "I am trapped, out of control, cannot make it stop," or "there is something wrong with me," we also see that they embraced additional *solution* beliefs about holding on to their anger and unforgiveness. It is these beliefs —and not their heart beliefs— which kept them emotionally entangled with their abuser. Beliefs such as "My not forgiving keeps him from getting by with what he did", "My not forgiving makes sure that others know the truth about what really happened," or "My not forgiving protects me from being hurt again" were common.

Each of their solution beliefs was arrived at because they were serving them in some manner. However, God's assessment of these same events is different from their own and His solution is knowing the truth.

After each of these women viewed their life experiences through the eyes of Christ, they could let go of their false interpretations and futile solutions and easily forgive the debt. At the end of the day, their memories were still the same, the injustice was still unjust, and the perpetrator was still guilty, and most were walking around free. However, the debt was forgiven, and the women themselves were free. Their forgiveness released the debt and released the one who was holding the mortgage.

---

*AT THE END OF THE DAY, THEIR MEMORIES WERE STILL THE SAME, THE INJUSTICE WAS STILL UNJUST, AND THE PERPETRATOR WAS STILL GUILTY AND WALKING AROUND FREE. HOWEVER, THE DEBT WAS FORGIVEN, AND THE WOMEN THEMSELVES WERE FREE.*

---

None of these women ever reconciled with the debtor. None of the debtors have yet come clean for what they did or sought reconciliation. Nonetheless, these women walked away free, and their abusers will someday give a full account to God.

### *Freedom in Central America*

Let me give you an extreme but true story of how this works. I have some good friends in Central America. They have been practicing TPM for many years along with a large group of others in their area. I was planning to do a seminar in their city, and was about to leave for the trip, when I received a phone call from them about a horrific event that had just taken place.

The mother of the family had just come home from work, pulled her car into her garage, and let the garage door down. She was unaware that an armed robber had come in with her while the door was open. Once the door closed, he pulled a gun on her.

He forced her into the house where her husband and two children were. Holding them all at gunpoint, he proceeded to open the front door, letting in six heavily armed men brandishing weapons. Now there were seven men in their house threatening to kill them. Their youngest child was sleeping in his bedroom, but their older daughter was not. The thugs forced the mother and father to get down into an execution position saying they were going to kill the daughter unless they told them where they kept all their valuables. They forced the daughter to take them through the house as they gathered the goods. During the entire ordeal, this family assumed that they were going to be killed.

After ransacking the house, the thieves made the daughter join her parents on the floor on their knees, covering them with a sheet. Based on conversation between the thugs and what they were doing, it appeared they were planning to execute the family.

As the family was quietly saying their last goodbyes, the leader of the gang suddenly said, "We need to get out of here." This command confused the rest of the gang, but they complied, and all ran out, leaving the family under the sheet wondering what had happened.

After a while they came out from under the sheet and realized that the ordeal was over. However, the emotional trauma that followed was overwhelming. Shortly thereafter, I arrived in their town with my son, Joshua. We immediately sought them out and offered care to them. All of them were greatly shaken and overwhelmed by the experience. We prayed with them using the TPM model.

For anyone who has not experienced TPM, what I am about to share may sound fabricated and exaggerated, but I am toning it down so that it is more believable. The point is, it is not what happens in a difficult life situation which causes the trauma that follows, but how it was perceived and interpreted. Post-traumatic stress is caused by the way traumatic events are perceived, not by the traumatic events themselves. It is the belief that is formed and established within the experience that becomes our heart belief that follows thereafter. This belief results in the overwhelming fear, panic, and anxiety.

I had the privilege of praying separately with the daughter and the mother, each in different settings. Neither had any idea of what occurred in the other's ministry session until both were completed. Both had interpreted the experience with beliefs such as "I am going to die," "I am trapped and out of control," and "I am helpless." (In TPM these would be defined as "State-of-Being" lies or our erroneous perception of God.) They also believed things such as "these men violated our family," "they destroyed our world and made it an unsafe place," and "we will never be the same." Their interpretation of what happened became the "debt" that they held, which kept them in emotional bondage and turmoil. To forgive this great debt would be impossible, since to do so would require going against what they experientially believed to be true.

Both mother and daughter had a wonderful encounter with the Lord in their separate ministry sessions. His truth freed them, so they could let go of the lie-based interpretations they had come to believe. Someone might say, "But it was true: they almost died, they were powerless, they were violated, their view of the world has changed, they should feel unsafe, and they will never be the same!" The only truth among these is the last one, "they will never be the same!" Because of this experience and the truth that God granted them, their family was transformed in very positive and powerful ways and they will indeed, never be the same.

When I ministered with the daughter and the mother, each of them reported a very similar memory recollection of the traumatic event. Both remembered believing they were going to die and remembered bracing themselves for the gunshots. However, they both remembered being surprised to hear the leader suddenly say, "We need to get out of here."

What I am about to share may be hard for some people to believe. I also have no way to verify if what occurred was valid, apart from the undeniable transformation that occurred in the lives of this mother and daughter. What they both reported next is something they each reported to have experienced in their hearts.

At this point in the ministry process, both said separately that they could see Jesus (with their mind's eye) standing in the room, poised, calm, and in complete control. They said they could hear Jesus commanding the leader, "You need to get out of here," and then the men scrambled to get out of the house. Jesus apparently revealed this individually to both mother and daughter and, at that moment, they each believed they were safe and totally protected. The lies they had believed about being killed, completely vanished as the safety and protection of Christ was realized. There were many more truths granted by the Spirit in later sessions that have literally transformed this family.

All family members have reported that to date, there is no trauma left in the memory of what happened to them that night. When they remember the event, they see the Lord watching over them and they believe He sent the thugs away exactly when they left. They believe that God used this life experience to bring about in them a lasting and eternal transformation. As I said earlier, it is all about the interpretation of the experience and not the experience itself.

The true interpretation of this event was that they were never in danger; Jesus was in complete control from beginning to end. It was never true that they almost died, even though at that moment they believed it to be true. They were not going to die; God protected them. They were powerless in their own strength, as is true for all of us, all the time, but His power was with them, even though they did not realize it. They were not violated. They were blessed and given the opportunity to see God in a way they had never seen Him before. Today they say they are eternally grateful for the experience and for the transformation God brought about in their lives through it. Interpretation—seeing life from God's perspective, not our own—is what it is all about.

Some may protest that feeling fearful is totally expected in a situation such as this. I would agree that I also would have been horrified, feeling helpless and without hope. But this doesn't mean that this would have been based upon the truth. My emotional state would have been totally dependent upon what I believed to be the truth in the moment. If I had God's heavenly perspective, my emotions would have matched His viewpoint. This is why Jesus was not afraid when He saw the cross before Him.

I believe that when Stephen was about to be stoned to death and saw the heavens open, revealing Jesus standing at the right hand of the Father, his emotions immediately changed to correspond with heaven's perspective. Just because the disciples caught in the stormy sea believed they were about to die and cried out, "Lord, do you not know we are about to perish?" did not mean they were about to drown. Their fear was based upon their perspective of the situation and not upon the truth.

At different times in my life I have been within one foot of a lion, a grizzly bear, a hippopotamus, a king cobra, and a fifteen-foot African crocodile. Each one of these creatures had the power and ability to kill me. Although I was within striking distance, I was never in any danger. I was at the zoo, separated from them by a sturdy barrier. In the same way, just because you have seven heavily armed robbers in your house does not necessarily mean that you are in danger, even though it seems to be so. Jesus stood as a barrier between them and any possible harm. Someone might ask, "But what if they had been killed?" Again, it is all perspective and how we view God and what He does or allows. The question is, can God be trusted? What we believe about this will determine what we feel in any given moment. Again, the Scriptures declare, *"May the Lord of peace Himself, grant you peace in <u>every</u> circumstance"* (2 Thess. 3:16). Had they been killed, I have to believe that it was their time to die and the Lord was with them. Sometimes very terrible things happen, but from a heavenly perspective and an eternal frame of reference, all things take on a different and true meaning.

When we all get to heaven none of us will be mad at God because of how He did or did not do what we had expected of Him. We will all be totally satisfied with His every decision. It is all about perspective.

### *Was the cross a bad thing?*

The cross of Jesus was a terrible event. However, from a heavenly perspective God might see it differently. The Scriptures says, *"...the LORD was <u>pleased</u> to crush Him, putting Him to grief; If He would render Himself as a guilt offering"* (Isa. 53:10). It depends on your interpretation.

Were any of the Apostles' executions a bad thing? They did not seem to think so. They saw it as an honor and a privilege. When Jesus was hanging on the cross, was He in danger? That depends upon your interpretation. Jesus said to the Roman soldiers about to arrest Him, *"...do you think that I cannot appeal to My Father, and He will at once put at My disposal more than twelve legions of angels?"* (Matt. 26:53). He declared that He could stop what was happening anytime He chose to. Because this was true and He knew it to be so, it was impossible for Him to feel afraid. Again, we always feel whatever we believe; ALWAYS.

Someone could ask, "What about the many innocent people—including children—who have been abused, unjustly treated, and even killed by wicked people? What happened to their protection?" That is a good question. We may have few logical answers to give, but there may be limitless explanations from God's perspective that we have yet to consider.

First, we must assume that we do not yet understand God's perspective in every case. It's also possible we will never know His perspective on everything in this life. We will always be looking *"...through a mirror dimly..."* (1 Cor. 13:12). However, when we cannot see with clarity, we can still believe, and therefore know that God can be trusted. He can be trusted to do what is right even when it seems that what He is doing or allowing is something we cannot comprehend. When our experiential belief is "I can trust God," then we do not have to know anything more.

### *God's Heart Versus His Mind*

God did not leave us without His word in this area. The Scriptures say clearly, *"His ways are not our ways and His thoughts are not our thoughts"* (Isaiah 55:8). Even though we may never know the mind of God while on this earth, He has been very clear concerning His heart. Whenever I do not know what

He is thinking, I can look to Calvary and see the Father's heart. He was willing to allow His Only Son to die on a cross for me. I may not comprehend His thinking in this, but I cannot deny His love for me.

*The Apostle Paul said,*

> *If God is for us, who is against us? He who did not spare His Own Son, but delivered Him over for us all, how will He not also with Him freely give us all things? ... Who will separate us from the love of Christ? Will tribulation, or distress, or persecution, or famine, or nakedness, or peril, or sword? ... For I am convinced that neither death, nor life, nor angels, nor principalities, nor things present, nor things to come, nor powers, nor height, nor depth, nor any other created thing, will be able to separate us from the love of God, which is in Christ Jesus our Lord. (excerpts from Rom. 8:31-39)*

This passage reveals the heart of God. We may never fully comprehend His mind, but we can observe and embrace His heart; His ways are not our ways and His thoughts are too great to fully comprehend. Just because our interpretation of a situation is that God has abandoned us, has rejected us, or is withholding good from us, doesn't make it so. The proof is the Cross.

---

**EVEN THOUGH WE MAY NEVER KNOW THE MIND OF GOD WHILE ON THIS EARTH, HE HAS BEEN VERY CLEAR CONCERNING HIS HEART. WHENEVER I DO NOT KNOW WHAT HE IS THINKING, I CAN LOOK TO CALVARY AND SEE THE FATHER'S HEART.**

---

I think of Jesus hanging from the cross. As He suffered this injustice and took on the debt of all our sins, He felt compassion. This is because He knew the truth. From truth and compassion, He prayed, "*...Father, forgive them for they know not what they do*" (Luke 23:34).

What is my response to a God who stands back and allows men to do very evil things? I probably don't have anything to say that hasn't already been said by many who have come before me. However, the suffering of the innocent has few logical human explanations. The theologians and philosophers have discussed this question endlessly. I personally believe there is only one reliable answer, and I quote again the scripture in which God has plainly spoken, "'*My thoughts are not your thoughts, nor are your ways My ways,' declares the LORD*" (Isa. 55:8).

---

*WHEN WE ALL GET TO HEAVEN NONE OF US WILL BE MAD AT GOD BECAUSE OF HOW HE DID OR DID NOT DO WHAT WE HAD EXPECTED OF HIM. WE WILL ALL BE TOTALLY SATISFIED WITH HIS EVERY DECISION. IT IS ALL ABOUT PERSPECTIVE.*

---

### *Two Options*

We have only two options: believe and trust God, or not. If we decide to trust God, the faith required to do so isn't something we can muster up. Faith is experiential and granted by God, and trust is the expected outcome of this. Trying harder to trust will not work. Trust is what we do only after we believe. Belief is something that we do because someone has persuaded us of the truth. We are back to the root meaning of faith; *peitho*. When God persuades me of the truth in my heart I believe. Because I believe I can trust.

It's only when I truly believe and trust God with absolute certainty that I can rest amid the storm and lie down beside Jesus who is asleep in the stern of the boat. If I don't have His perspective and, instead, come up with my own interpretation, such as, "I am going to die," I will cry out like the disciples, "*Lord, do you not know we are about to perish?*" (Luke 8:24). The truth is, the disciples were never anywhere near death. They were in the same boat and storm as Jesus, and yet He was asleep.

### *There are several opinions concerning the question of God's involvement in this world.*

Some are as follows:

- There is no God, and life just randomly happens.
- There is a God, but He is not involved.
- There is a God, but He acts randomly and is unpredictable, in that sometimes He helps, and sometimes He doesn't.
- There is a God, but He is a little twisted and is playing a game with all of us.
- There is a God who is good and is always involved, but we cannot comprehend His ways.

This last opinion is the one that I hold.

The bottom line is simple. God is good and is all-powerful and can do anything He chooses, whenever He chooses. Therefore, anything He chooses to do is good. What God permits to occur may come from the hands of evil people. It is not His will that people choose evil, but it is His will that people choose freely. It is not God's intention that the innocent suffer because of the choices that evil people make, but it is His will that free will should exist.

So, does this mean that it's God's will that innocent children suffer from evil abuse? Not at all. To the contrary, it breaks His heart. Their suffering is not His will, but rather it is an outcome of the free will that was created and ordained by Him. It is God's will that people have freedom to choose, but His intention for granting free will is that people might choose to do good and not *evil*.

---

*IT IS GOD'S WILL THAT PEOPLE HAVE FREEDOM TO CHOOSE, BUT HIS INTENTION FOR GRANTING FREE WILL IS THAT PEOPLE MIGHT CHOOSE TO DO GOOD AND NOT EVIL.*

---

When we do not choose good, He allows it, since it is His will that people choose freely. If He stops a person from choosing evil, where does God draw the line for any of us? This is the price paid because of the free will He has allowed us to have. But there is also great benefit. When He allows us to exercise free will, it enables us to have a genuine relationship with Him. Without the freedom to choose God or reject Him, there can be no relationship.

This is what separates us from all other living things. Animals follow their instincts or behave as they are trained. They really do not make free-will choices. Geese fly south in the winter because their instincts tell them to. We do not have to follow our instincts; instead we make decisions. We can choose to love or hate, give or take, speak truth or lies, blame others or take ownership of our own problems. Free will allows us to interact relationally with God in love.

However, the consequence of free will is that injustice abounds. Does this injustice go unnoticed by God? Not at all. All injustice will be fully dealt with in eternity. Is there any hope or benefit for those who have suffered unjustly? Yes, indeed, but this cannot be realized apart from a true interpretation of events by viewing them from heaven's perspective. When God grants us His perspective of the injustices we have suffered, we see that the benefits far outweigh the trouble. Paul said it this *way, "...for momentary, light affliction is producing for us an eternal weight of glory far beyond all comparison…"* (2 Cor. 4:17).

God has always used the evil acts of people *"to work for our good"* (Rom. 8:28). God has a well-thought-out plan that takes into account anything evil people do to us, and this is affirmed by the passage that says, *"if God be for us who can be against us?"* Since God is *for us*, everything that evil men may do becomes *for us* as well.

Though we may have many options to explain why "bad things happen to good people," I believe there is only one that has biblical merit. God is God and does what He does because He IS. We are incapable of even minutely comprehending His ways and will never scratch the surface in understanding His thinking. As I already stated, God made this clear through the prophet Isaiah where He said, *"For as the heavens are higher than the earth, so are My ways higher than your ways and My thoughts than your thoughts"* (Isa. 55:9). No matter how much God allows us to know about Himself, there will always *remain a*n infinite measure of knowledge that will remain unknown.

If you will, remember the account of Job. This is exactly the position he finally came to regarding God. God is God and can be trusted even though we cannot comprehend His ways. Genuine faith can be summed up in the words of Job when he said, concerning the difficulties that God had brought upon him, *"Though he slay me, yet will I trust in him…"* (Job 13:15). Job did not understand God, but he trusted him.

It is impossible to know Him in any full measure since we cannot comprehend or contain infinite knowledge, but then we do not need *to do so. He has not called us to know Him in this manner, rather, He has called us to trust His heart and rely upon His faithfulness.* His heart was revealed to us in Jesus and the ultimate sacrifice He made in love for us. This understanding can only come about as we are persuaded by God of the truth within our hearts. This persuasion is faith and only brought about by God. So then may the *"...God of our Lord Jesus Christ, the Father of glory... give to you a spirit of wisdom and of revelation in the knowledge of Him. I pray that the eyes of your heart may be enlightened, so that you will know what is the hope of His calling..."* (Eph. 1:*17-18*).

# *Discussion Questions*

1. Read again this passage: "The king "released him and forgave him the debt, but that slave went out and found one of his fellow slaves who owed him a hundred denarii; and he seized him" (Matt. 18:27-28). What do the two words "released" and "seized" say to us about the necessity of forgiveness?

2. What is your response to the idea that *"forgiveness does NOT have the power to change the one being forgiven, but it will change the one who is doing the forgiving?"*

3. How can knowing the heart of God—as opposed to understanding the thoughts and ways of God—answer the question *"Why does God allow bad things to happen* to good people?"

4. There are several opinions concerning this question. *Some are as follows:*

   - *There is no God, and life just randomly happens.*
   - *There is a God, but He is not involved.*
   - *There is a God, but He acts randomly and is unpredictable, in that sometimes He helps and sometimes He doesn't.*
   - *There is a God, but He is a little twisted and is playing a game with all of us.*
   - *There is a God who is good and is always involved, but we cannot comprehend His ways.*

5. Which of these options do you most agree with and why? Do you have another option that might be considered?

*Chapter Eleven: Principle Six: Forgiveness emotionally releases the one offering the forgiveness ...*

# Chapter Twelve

## Principle Seven: Forgiveness should not be confused with reconciliation

Forgiveness is sometimes confused with reconciliation. They are not the same. Forgiveness focuses on the debt; reconciliation is relational and focuses on restoration. Forgiveness is totally within the control of the one forgiving and does not require the debtor to be present, to cooperate, or even want to be forgiven. Reconciliation, however, requires that the one in debt takes full responsibility for what he has done, appeals with a broken and contrite heart to the one he has wounded, and seeks to restore the relationship.

The one holding the "mortgage" can forgive whether the debtor seeks forgiveness or not. However, he cannot bring about reconciliation without the other party choosing to be reconciled. The power to forgive lies solely with the one forgiving, whereas reconciliation does not. Reconciliation is only possible when both parties agree and desire it.

Remember, the New Testament Greek word for forgive is apheimy. This word means to cut off, separate, release, or remove something. Forgiveness can be given regardless of whether reconciliation ever takes place. Remember, when God forgives, He does not forgive (cut off) the person, but rather He cuts off the sin, or debt. We, too, can cut off the debt owed us, even without reconciling with the person, but we can never be reconciled unless the person who hurt us desires this and is willing to work towards it.

The good news is that God is not only interested in forgiving (canceling out) our debt of sin, He also desires that we be reconciled to Him. To those who have believed, "*He has now reconciled you in His fleshly body through death, to present you before Him holy and blameless and beyond reproach*" (Col. 1:22).

There is no indication in Matthew 18 that the King and the servant ever became friends, ate lunch together, or sat with each other in church. As a matter of fact, there is no indication in Scripture that their relationship ever improved from the day the servant was called in to give an account. Yet, at the first meeting, the King truly released the servant and forgave him his debt.

My banker could call me (probably will not) and inform me that he has made the decision to cancel all my debts. It really doesn't matter if I'm happy, grateful, desirous, or even willing to receive this gift. If he chooses to release me of the debt, I have no choice but to be released. I can scream, cuss, or protest loudly. I can tell him I will not accept it. I can even continue to send in my monthly payments, but the bottom line is that I owe nothing to the bank if the banker decides to tear up my note.

To summarize, the power to forgive lies totally in the hands of the one who holds the note. The one in debt has no influence over whether or not forgiveness occurs. Reconciliation, however, is a separate issue, and the two should never be confused. Forgiveness is letting go of the debts others owe you. Reconciliation is restoration of the relationship. I can forgive you (release you of your debt) whether you want me to or not, but I cannot be truly reconciled to you until you accept responsibility for your sin, confess the error of your ways, and in penitent brokenness, seek to restore our relationship. The servant in the story pretended to be broken and contrite, but this was not his true condition. Therefore, there is no mention of reconciliation in the story.

---

***FORGIVENESS IS LETTING GO OF THE DEBTS OTHERS OWE YOU.***
***RECONCILIATION IS RESTORATION OF THE RELATIONSHIP.***

---

Paul says, "*If possible, so far as it depends on you, be at peace with all men*" (Rom. 12:18). Bottom line? Not everyone wants to be reconciled, and we cannot always be at peace with all people. Reconciliation is based upon relationship, which will not happen when an offender refuses to do the right thing and be reconciled. You can still forgive that person and love him with the love of Christ, but if he refuses to take responsibility, no reconciliation will occur.

In relationships where forgiveness is needed, such as in a marriage, both parties are usually holding debts toward the other. Unless they can let the debts go, reconciliation cannot occur. One of them may forgive and be free to love, but complete reconciliation is not possible unless both take responsibility for their wrongdoing and freely release the other from theirs.

Marital conflict is rarely about the two people involved. It is almost always about the lie-based pain of each being triggered and the projection of blame onto the other. Because this is the case, each person will need to cease blaming their spouse by taking full responsibility for their own pain, before forgiveness and reconciliation can occur.

### *A Twist at the End of the Story*

There is a twist at the end of the story we have been looking at. When the king heard about the servant's unwillingness to forgive his fellow servant, he turned him over to the torturers until he could pay back the full amount.

What happened to the king's forgiveness? There are several things that need to be considered here, but first let's look at the passage.

> "So, when his fellow slaves saw what had happened, they were deeply grieved and came and reported to their lord all that had happened. Then summoning him, his lord said to him, 'You wicked slave, I forgave you all that debt because you pleaded with me. Should you not also have had mercy on your fellow slave, in the same way that I had mercy on you?' And his lord, moved with anger, handed him over to the torturers until he should repay all that was owed him. My heavenly Father will also do the same to you, if each of you does not forgive his brother from your heart" (Matt. 18:31-35).

First, in order to understand the twist at the end of Jesus' narrative, we must understand the context in which it was being told. Jesus was teaching God's perfect standard of forgiveness. By raising the standard of the Law to its proper and perfect level, all of His listeners were condemned because none of them had perfectly and completely forgiven their debtors *"...from the heart."*

As Jesus described within the narrative, "[the king being] *...moved with anger, handed him over to the torturers until he should repay all that he owed him.* "My heavenly Father will also do the same to you, *if each of you does not forgive his brother from your heart." (Matt. 18:34-35)*

These words were not encouraging to the disciples, but rather words of hopeless despair for all who heard them. Nonetheless, this is the reality of the standard of perfection that the Law requires that no man can achieve. Thank God for grace.

We, too, are lacking, but yet, we are under grace. Jesus came to fulfill the holy requirements of the Law and has offered us full forgiveness of all our sin, past, present and future. Because of grace there is *"... now no condemnation for those who are in Christ"* (Rom. 8:1). Because we are made right with God and all our sins forgiven, we can now *"... Be kind to one another, tenderhearted, forgiving each other, just as God in Christ also has forgiven you"* (Eph. 4:32).

This teaching in Matthew 18 is one of the many difficult teachings of Jesus that must be understood through the lens of the Law as opposed to grace. When the disciples heard these words, they were not encouraged; they were shocked beyond belief and sorely discouraged.

It was teachings such as this that left them scratching their heads more than once. In another place where Jesus expounded on the difficulty for a rich man to get into heaven, the disciples were dumbfounded. The passage says, *"When the disciples heard this, they were very astonished and said, 'Then who can be saved?'"* (Matt. 19:25). The Greek word translated "astonished" in this verse is *ekplssō* that means to be literally knocked out of one's senses or thrown into a panic.

These words were terrifying and fearful. Peter couldn't have walked away feeling good about himself after hearing the Lord's words concerning forgiveness. If anything, he felt immense pressure to try to forgive "from his heart" 490 times! Only a fool would desire to be placed under such a demanding requirement, or worse, think that he might accomplish it. Jesus' words here clearly expressed the impossible task of a person being able to forgive apart from the intervention of God. Jesus' words also expressed the wonder and splendor of God's forgiveness for those who have no means to repay. It is clear that true forgiveness only comes from a heart that God has persuaded of the truth. It is not something we can do simply by our choosing to.

### *The Law is not, nor was it ever our friend.*

The Law is good and perfect, but it does not work in our favor. The Law is a taskmaster, always demanding perfection, which is impossible to attain

(Gal. 3:24). There is no room for any slacking off when we are under the Law. If we miss one *"jot or tittle"* (Matt. 5:18) in keeping the Law, we are guilty of breaking it all. The Law is "all or nothing," "pass or fail," and nothing in between. Paul said this concerning the Law, *"...when the commandment came, sin became alive and I died... the very commandment that was intended to bring life actually brought death"* (Rom. 7:9-10).

---

*THE LAW IS GOOD AND PERFECT, BUT IT DOES NOT WORK IN OUR FAVOR. IT IS A TASKMASTER, ALWAYS DEMANDING PERFECTION, WHICH IS IMPOSSIBLE TO ATTAIN (GAL. 3:24). THERE IS NO ROOM FOR ANY SLACKING OFF WHEN WE ARE UNDER THE LAW.*

---

The Lord's Prayer reflects a standard of forgiveness that many of us may have never actually considered. It is reminiscent of the Lord's words in Matthew 18:34-35 where he warned his disciples about the consequences of not fully forgiving from the heart. He said this concerning the King, *"In anger his master handed him over to the jailers to be tortured, until he should pay back all he owed. 'This is how my heavenly Father will treat each of you unless you forgive your brother or sister from your heart.'"*

As much as people like to quote the Lord's prayer during funerals and other special services saying, *"forgive us our sins <u>as we</u> forgive others,"* do we really want God to answer it according to what it says? Do you want God to forgive you according to the measure that you have forgiven others? If we would slow things down and seriously consider what we are asking of God in this prayer, we might reconsider how we pray. Are we really willing for God to forgive us as we have forgiven others? We are fine with most of the Lord's Prayer, that is, *"give us our daily bread, ... lead us not into temptation but deliver us from evil...."* but when we get down to the forgiving part, we may want to rethink our request. We may want to pray, "Thank you God that your forgiveness is based upon grace and not based upon the measure of our forgiving others."

The good news is this: Jesus taught this prayer in the context of the Law and was stressing the impossible standard that the Law demanded. His point was that it is impossible to forgive the way that God forgives unless it is "Christ in us" doing the forgiving. The good news is, we are under grace and His forgiveness is not contingent upon ours! It is also possible for us to forgive as He has forgiven when we know the truth with our hearts as He knew the truth. This is the goal of mind renewal: transformation (Rom. 12:2). Always keep in mind that mind renewal is a work of God and not a pursuit of knowledge.

So then, there is nothing encouraging about what the Lord says here: *"Forgive us our debts as we have forgiven our debtors."* Have you completely forgiven every offense that you have held against every person throughout your life? I hope so, but then I am placing all my "hope so" in the finished work of Christ. Thanks be to God for His grace. How much better is the grace of God on the victorious side of the cross! I personally do not want God to forgive me based upon how well I have forgiven others. I want mercy and grace, not justice.

So, when we get to this part of the story, Jesus points out the consequence of the servant's failure to forgive. It's not good, and Peter is probably wishing he had never asked the Lord this question in the first place. The "seventy times seven" is suddenly made clear; either we forgive completely and continually as God forgives, or we can expect terrible consequences—we will be "handed over to the torturers until we can pay back all that is owed!" However, there is hope in this terrible place. Rather than God forgiving us according to how we have forgiven, Jesus' story compares and contrasts our unwillingness and inability to forgive with God the Father's grace and all sufficiency. Again, thank the Lord for grace!

## *Summary of Basic Principles*

Keeping the original intent of the narrative in focus, there are a couple of principles we can glean from this part of the story. Some have already been alluded to earlier, but I will reiterate:

1. The attitude and character of the one in debt is irrelevant when it comes to forgiveness. We can forgive the debt no matter the attitude or heart condition of the debtor.

2. There is no reason to expect change in those who have been forgiven of their debt. Forgiving a person's debt typically has little or no impact on either their taking ownership for what they have done or changing their behavior.

3. There are times when people need to be called to account for the sins they have committed. We are instructed to forgive, and doing so greatly benefits the one forgiving, but sometimes it is also important for offenders to be held accountable for their actions.

This is especially true when there is the potential that others may be hurt. When a child or elderly person has been abused, there are legal requirements to report that information, whether the offender has been forgiven or not. Without question "*...love covers a multitude of sins...*" (1 Pet. 4:8), but not when others are put in harm's way.

For most relational situations where forgiveness is extended, holding a person accountable for their debt is not necessary. As the Apostle Peter said, "*...above all, keep fervent in your love for one another, because love covers a multitude of sins*" (1 Pet. 4:8). For example, when it comes to my relationship with my wife, she is quick to forgive me and does not hold the debt over my head. The love she has for me has allowed her to overlook many of my "sins" through the years.

However, she has also held me accountable at times. There are some sins for which people need to be held accountable. When I forget to take my shoes off at the door and I track mud across the floor my wife has just cleaned, it creates a "debt." But this is a debt she can generally make mention of (call me to account), forgive, and cover over with her love. I think you get my *point.*

### Forgive? Always. Confront? Your Call.

I used to believe that a part of total recovery from having been abused was confronting one's abuser. At that time, I believed that as victims of abuse became emotionally stable and strong, they would need to confront and hold their abusers accountable. Somehow, I believed that doing this would empower the victim. I now see this is not necessary. As people come into perfect peace, they can view their abusers through the eyes of Christ, with genuine compassion and forgiveness. True freedom comes from this, and not through confrontation.

I used to encourage victims to connect with what I thought was their righteous anger and use it as strength to face those who had hurt them. Today I neither encourage nor discourage confrontation. If the person feels the need to confront, I first want them to discern what is driving their need to do so. If there is any negative emotion behind what they are feeling compelled to do, we assume there is a lie-based belief that needs to be resolved before proceeding in that direction.

If they have anger, revenge, or any other negative emotion, I encourage them to continue pursuing their own freedom until they can confront with perfect peace and compassion. When we are able to confront from a position of peace rather than anger, the impact on the one accused of the abuse can be incredible. Confrontation is much more effective when done in the peace the Lord gives rather than in anger. I have noticed, however, when people find their own freedom, confrontation becomes less important to them.

Way back in 1995 when I was operating a counseling ministry, the members of my sexual abuse survivors' group were some of the first recipients of TPM. Linda (not her real name) was a young lady who had worked very hard for several years with me. She finally experienced freedom as we used TPM to identify her lie-based beliefs. Linda had been abused by her grandfather many times as a little girl. Before she underwent TPM, the very thought of confronting him caused her to feel small and powerless. Prior to using TPM, we had practiced the potential confrontation many times in group sessions through role-playing and talking to empty chairs, but Linda made very little progress in this area.

As we began to apply the process of TPM, she became less and less fearful and the feelings of powerlessness vanished as her lies were replaced with truth. She said it was as though she was growing up on the inside as the Lord replaced each lie with His truth. She reported feeling increasingly adult rather than continually feeling like a little child. When she thought of the abusive memories, she felt strong and confident and had perfect peace.

One evening Linda called me at my home. She was very emotional when she first started speaking, and I thought she was having a crisis and needed help. It suddenly occurred to me that she was excited, not upset. She went on to say, "Well, I did it!" I had no idea what she had done, so I asked, "Did what?" She went on to tell me that she had just confronted her grandfather. Just by chance she had come face-to-face with him in the city park earlier that same day.

When she saw him, she had expected to feel childlike, fearful, and overwhelmed. Instead, she had felt no fear or panic, but only calmness and confidence. She walked over to him and proceeded to confront him with what he had done to her. She had not felt angry, small, or fearful, and she was not acting out of revenge. She was simply letting him know that the secret was out and that he was going to have to face it and its consequences.

Although he denied what he had done after she finished telling him all she wanted to say, his response didn't bother her. She simply restated the facts with the same adult-like confidence. When he saw that she was unwavering, he began to panic, expressed fear of being put in jail, and begged her not to tell anyone. She told him that at this point she had forgiven him and would leave the consequences of his crime to God and move on with her life. She also let him know that her forgiveness did not release him from being responsible for his actions in relation to God or to those whom he had hurt.

Later she did report his crimes to some members of the family whom she suspected had been hurt by him. Her sister and several cousins came forward with similar stories of their grandfather's abuse. Her freedom brought about freedom for many others.

I am not suggesting whether or not victims should confront their abusers. This is their own choice. *However, I do STRONGLY suggest that no confrontation takes place until it can be done in genuine freedom* and peace. In cases where children or the elderly are in harm's way, then everything should be done to protect them.

When people come to know the truth, they will do what previously seemed impossible because they have let go of their lie-based interpretations of what happened to them. With genuine heartfelt compassion, they are able to forgive those who have hurt them. The Lord's peace and compassion replaces their anger, bitterness, and resentment toward those who have hurt them. They are then free to see their abusers through the eyes of Christ. Jesus truly loves the vilest of sinners and desires their complete redemption. When we receive His eyes, we are released to love with His love.

Forgiveness will occur without struggle or effort when the person is free from the lies he believes. When the Lord gives the wounded person "His eyes" to view the one in debt from a heavenly perspective, forgiveness will follow. Forgiveness should be viewed as a result of personal freedom and evidenced by compassion. Forgiveness is not the goal, but the expected outcome of freedom.

Someone might ask if forgiveness is the outcome of one's personal freedom or the compassion one feels toward those who have hurt us, then what comes first, our freedom or compassion? God must first release us of our lie-based belief before we can view the person and his offense in truth. Compassion is the natural outcome of our viewing the person and his offense through the eyes of Christ in truth. When we know the truth in our hearts, compassion will follow. Our belief determines what we feel toward those who have hurt us and not the offense or debt they have with us.

When Jesus was hanging on the cross He was abiding in perfect truth. Because He viewed His abusers through the truth, He expressed compassion for those who were crucifying Him. When *He said, "Father, forgive them; for they do not know what they are doing"* (Lu. 23:34), He expressed compassion through *truth*.

---

*COMPASSION IS THE NATURAL OUTCOME OF OUR VIEWING THE PERSON AND HIS OFFENSE THROUGH THE EYES OF CHRIST IN TRUTH. WHEN WE KNOW THE TRUTH IN OUR HEARTS, COMPASSION WILL FOLLOW.*

---

When the person is free from the lie-based thinking he harbored, he can forgive without effort; that is, he can let go, sever, or *cut off* (apheimy) the wrong done to him. In this place of release, there will be the presence of compassion from which the forgiveness is expressed. "The king felt compassion and forgave him his debt." Remember that we are not talking here about reconciliation, which can only occur in the rare cases where the one who was in "debt" takes ownership and genuinely seeks restoration. The focus of forgiveness is the release of a debt, not the restoration of a relationship.

To feel compassion is to feel what the Lord feels towards the person who needs his forgiveness. The Lord felt compassion when He looked down from the cross at those who were abusing him. This is why He could say, *"Father, forgive them..."* As James the Apostle declared, *"...the Lord is full of compassion and is merciful"* (Ja. 5:11).

Keep in mind that it is common to hold many "debts" towards the same person. Each one must be taken into account as each debt may be supported by its own lie-based beliefs. Because this is so, a general approach to forgiveness is rarely successful. However, as each lie is replaced with the truth, compassion will arise. Where there is compassion, forgiveness follows naturally and without effort.

## *Discussion Questions*

1. What is the difference between forgiveness and reconciliation? How is it possible to completely forgive and yet never be reconciled?

2. Why is it important to view the last part of Matthew 18 within its context of the Law and Old Covenant with God? We all honor and respect the Ten Commandments, but in what way are they not our friend?

3. If it is sometimes appropriate and necessary to confront someone for their past deeds, when should we do this and why?

*Chapter Twelve: Principle Seven: Forgiveness should not be confused with reconciliation*

# Final Words

## Forgiveness allows us to see the bigger picture

For those of you who are using the TPM ministry (or considering using it) as a ministry model to follow when helping others and for your own personal journey with God, there is a bigger picture than the immediate freedom that God grants us in a ministry session. We define the purpose of TPM as *"a means by which we are able to willfully and intentionally participate with what God is doing to refine our faith, renew our minds and transform our lives."*

---

*TPM IS "A MEANS BY WHICH WE ARE ABLE TO WILLFULLY AND INTENTIONALLY PARTICIPATE WITH WHAT GOD IS DOING TO REFINE OUR FAITH, RENEW OUR MINDS AND TRANSFORM OUR LIVES."*

---

In TPM we seek to reframe the hurtful and unjust things that come our way as the refiner's fire purifying our faith, as opposed to simply being something to endure and get through. Life crises and difficulties provide the context in which God is able to do His greatest work in us, if we cooperate with Him in it. As badly as we may have been treated, abused, or neglected by those around us, God is greater than all of this. He has a plan for us and He will complete it. Nothing anyone may do can hinder His handiwork.

The writer of Hebrews uses the analogy of a father disciplining a son to make this same point. He says this: *"... All discipline for the moment seems not to be joyful, but sorrowful; yet to those who have been trained by it, afterwards it yields the peaceable fruit of righteousness"* (Heb. 12:11). No one likes the refiner's fire, but for those who are trained by it, there is great benefit. However, for those who are not trained by it, it can be a drudgery and purposeless heartache.

There is no question that people do bad things to innocent, undeserving people. When this occurs, damage is done, and unnecessary injustices take place. It is in these moments that we develop lie-based beliefs and erect solution beliefs in order to protect ourselves. We also lock the doors to forgiveness, making it impossible to experience our own freedom. However, if we can discover the big picture, we will see God in the midst of every fire that we have had to endure.

In an Old Testament account, Shadrach, Meshach and Abednego refused to bow down to the King and landed in the fiery furnace. Amazingly, the fire did not hurt them; it only burned off the cords with which they were bound. However, after they were in the heat for a time the King noticed there were not three in the fire, but four, and he cried out, *"Look! I see four men loosed and walking about in the midst of the fire without harm, and the appearance of the fourth is like a son of the gods!"* God is in the midst of the flame with us refining our faith.

The Apostle Paul discovered the bigger picture concerning his continual mistreatment, such as imprisonments, beatings, and being stoned and left for dead, because he understood that *"God causes all things to work together for those who love God, who are called according to His purpose"* (Rom. 8:28) and that *"if God be for us who can be against us?"* Rom. 8:31). Paul was able to *"exult in his tribulations"* (Rom. 5:3), because he knew the greater benefit.

It is wrong for people to do evil and unjust things to us, but God is greater than the wrong. It was wrong when evil men plotted against Christ and had him crucified unjustly. However, their injustice was instrumental in the Father's greater plan, His plan to make redemption available to the world.

The Apostle Paul was encouraging the church at Philippi, telling them not to worry about his imprisonment. He saw the bigger picture. This is partly why he wrote to them saying, *"... Now I want you to know, brothers and sisters, that what has happened to me has actually served to advance the gospel. As a result, it has become clear throughout the whole palace guard and to everyone else that I am in chains for Christ. And because of my chains, most of the brothers and sisters have become confident in the Lord and dare all the more to proclaim the gospel without fear"* (Phil. 1:13-14). Paul's chains were the means by which the Gospel was advancing, and the brothers were being made more confident to preach the Word.

As we come into our own freedom and can release others from their debts, our eyes will more fully open and we will see the bigger picture of what God is doing. He is using the hurts, injustices and difficulties we have experienced to refine us, renew us, and transform us. Our place is to position ourselves to receive what He has for us. He desires to persuade our hearts of the truth so that we may know Him and bear fruit in every good work. Amen, and amen.

### *What will you do?*

You may have people in your life toward whom you are angry, bitter, or resentful. If they hurt you unjustly, they were wrong. However, the fact that you feel what you feel is an indication that you have not yet been able to forgive and are still enmeshed. What are you going to do with this pain?

You may believe the anger protects you from further abuse or harm. This is not true. You may believe that if you forgive your abuser, he or she will be getting away with the crime. This also is not true. The anger, hate, and desire for revenge you hold is stealing the good things God has for you. He will go with you as you choose to search out and expose the lies you believe, and He will grant you His truth. He is very willing to relieve you of all the anger and resentment if you will allow Him to do so.

Though it may seem impossible or even impractical to forgive, you can. However, you will not likely do so by just choosing to. Forgiveness is the outcome of God granting us freedom from the lies we believe that keep us from being able to forgive. When we know the truth with our hearts, we can forgive from the heart.

If you are in emotional bondage to someone who has hurt you, I encourage you to seek ministry from someone who understands the TPM principles or knows how to help you to identify the lies that keep you from forgiving. Once you accurately identify the lies you believe, you will be able to go to Jesus for His truth. You can *"cast all your anxieties on Him, for He cares about you"* (1 Pet. 5:7, RSV).

We also encourage you to equip yourself with the knowledge that is available to you on the TPM website. Invest in your own freedom by choosing to learn the principles and concepts that have been introduced to you in this book. The Lord desires that you know the truth with your heart so that you *might "…be filled with the knowledge of His will in all spiritual wisdom and understanding, so that you will walk in a manner worthy of the Lord, to please Him in all respects, bearing fruit in every good work and increasing in the knowledge of God…"* (Col. 1:9-10) and finally, *"…May the Lord of peace Himself grant you peace in every circumstance"* (2 Thessalonians 3:16).

# Free Training in Transformation Prayer Ministry

Throughout this book you have been exposed to a ministry model called Transformation Prayer Ministry (TPM). TPM is one means by which many people are participating with God as He refines their faith, renews their minds and transforms their lives. He does this by exposing their lie-based belief and shining His light of truth into their hearts (2 Cor. 4:6).

It is heart belief that dictates how we view life and to a great extent how we will respond to what is happening in our world. However, as our heart belief is brought into the knowledge of the truth through the Spirit's persuasion, we will be transformed by this illumination, resulting in our experiencing the effortless expression of the fruit of the Spirit. The fruit of the Spirit is the outcome of knowing the truth in our hearts not a "To-Do" list to accomplish. It was heart belief in truth that brought us into the saving knowledge of Christ (Rom. 10:10) and it is heart belief in truth that will transform us into His likeness (Rom.8:29)

You are encouraged to continue your study in TPM. Training in this ministry model is freely available to you and your church online at www.transformationprayer.org. Go to the training area on the website and select the INTRODUCTION link to get started. You are also encouraged to leave comments about this book on the comment page provided on the website.